# THE NEW YORK PUBLIC LIBRARY AMAZING SCIENTISTS

## A Book of Answers for Kids

Jim Callan

A Stonesong Press Book

John Wiley & Sons, l

New York

To Polly . . .
my amazing discovery

This book is printed on acid-free paper. ∞

Published by John Wiley & Sons, Inc.
Published simultaneously in Canada.

This publication is designed to provide accurate and authoritative information in regard to the subject matter covered. It is sold with the understanding that the Publisher is not engaged in rendering legal, accounting, or other professional services. If legal advice or other expert assistance is required, the services of a competent professional person should be sought.

ISBN 0-471-39289-8

Printed in the United States of America

10 9 8 7 6 5 4 3 2 1

# CONTENTS

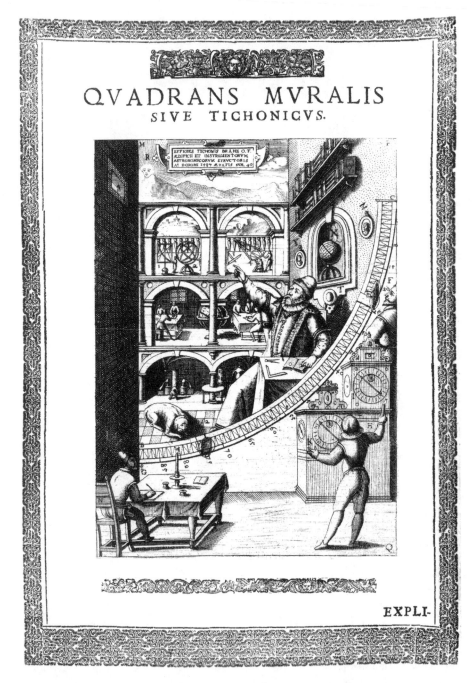

This 1587 depiction of Tycho Brahe in his observatory shows the astronomer pointing to the innovative instruments used in his work, such as a quadrant, a sextant, and an armillary sphere.

# INTRODUCTION

Which founder of chemistry died by the guillotine during the French Revolution? Which physicist discovered the laws of gravity, motion, and optics while he was on a break from college and didn't reveal his findings for 20 years? Which Greek scientist held off an invasion by the mighty Roman Empire with his ingenious inventions? Which astronomer made discoveries so threatening he was nearly condemned to death?

These are just a few of the questions answered in *The New York Public Library Amazing Scientists: A Book of Answers for Kids*. In the following pages, you'll be introduced to some of the greatest scientists of the last 2,500 years. Some were ridiculed for their theories. Some offended the religious beliefs of their time. A few died in their search for the truths of science. The history of science has been an amazing journey and we can only tell you some of the stories in these pages. To learn more, a good place to look is the New York Public Library or your local library.

From the beginning, humans have tried to understand their world and their universe by asking questions. Why does the Sun appear to move in the sky? Why are there mountains? At first, the answers were pretty fanciful. The Sun was carried by a giant boat on a great river. The mountains were there to hold up the sky. Many different gods and goddesses were thought to control the workings of nature. An ancient science, astrology, theorized that the stars and planets caused many events on Earth.

These beliefs lasted for thousands of years, but some people wanted more than beliefs; they wanted to know the truth. *Science* comes from the Latin word meaning "to know." The scientists in this book kept asking questions until they could discover the truth. More questions remain. How did the universe begin? What is the cure for cancer? They await the work of future scientists to find the amazing answers.

What was the ancient world? ◆ Who was Aristotle? ◆ Why is Aristotle considered the father of Biology? ◆ What was Aristotle's most important scientific contribution? ◆ What were Aristotle's contributions to astronomy and physics? ◆ Who was Hippocrates? ◆ How did Hippocrates change medical diagnosis and treatment? ◆ What Hippocratic ideas remain in practice today? ◆ What is the Hippocratic oath ◆ Who was Archimedes? ◆ What is the Archimedes screw? ◆ Did Archimedes really once run through the streets of Syracuse naked yelling "Eureka! Eureka!"? ◆ How did Archimedes single-handedly hold off the entire Roman

# SCIENTISTS OF THE ANCIENT WORLD

## What was the ancient world?

There is no exact date when the period known as the ancient world began. There are, however, two important developments that mark the transition of mankind's history from prehistoric to ancient: farming and written language.

Around 8000 B.C., the human lifestyle started to change as people learned to be farmers. Before this, most humans roamed the Earth, hunting animals and gathering food. When the food supply in one area ran out, they would move on to another area.

The development of farming meant people were settling in one area rather than moving around. The areas settled by these new farmers were in warm and fertile river valleys, where crops would grow well. Some of the earliest farmers settled in an area called the Fertile Crescent, which included the valleys of the Nile, Tigris, and Euphrates Rivers in what is now Egypt and Iraq.

As farming populations grew, cities developed. People now had time to do more than simply survive. They built homes and places of worship, they formed governments, and they shared beliefs. As the people in different cities cooperated, civilizations (from the Latin for "living in cities") like Egypt and Mesopotamia emerged.

Crafts like stonework and cloth weaving developed, so there were products to trade with nearby civilizations. The trading of goods led to two great inventions in the 3000s B.C.: the wheel and written language. With the wheel, people could transport their goods. With written language, they could communicate and share knowledge.

From 3000 B.C. to 1000 B.C., civilizations developed throughout the world—in India, China, the Americas, and Africa. The greatest of these was Greece. Starting around 600 B.C., Greece prospered because of its expertise in crafts, trade, and agriculture. This made possible tremendous advances in literature, architecture, mathematics, and science. Greek scholars studied nature to discover how it worked. Most of the scientists in this chapter are Greek.

The Roman Empire conquered Greece in 146 B.C. The Romans tried to continue the tradition of Greek learning, but their strength was in government and the military. Their empire grew so huge that it became impossible to manage. Rome fell to German barbarian tribes in A.D. 476. This event is usually considered the end of the ancient world and the beginning of the Middle Ages.

### Who was Aristotle?

Several Greek thinkers who lived between the sixth century B.C. and the second century A.D. are considered the world's first scientists. While most scholars of their time relied on religion and myths to explain how nature worked, these Greek thinkers used observation and logic. The most influential of these new scientists was Aristotle. Even his wrong ideas were still accepted centuries after his death.

*Plato realized Aristotle was a special student. He nicknamed him Anagnostes, which means "the Brain."*

Aristotle was born in 384 B.C. in Macedonia in northern Greece. When he was 17, he went to Athens to study at the Academy, the ancient world's first university, founded in 387 B.C. by the great Greek scholar and educator Plato. Aristotle was deeply influenced by Plato's ideas on the formation of the universe, the composition of celestial bodies, and the forces creating the movements of these bodies.

After Plato's death, Aristotle returned to Macedonia and became the tutor to the Macedonian king's son,

Alexander. It was the most important job Aristotle would ever have. Alexander loved his teacher, and when he later ruled the world as Alexander the Great, he made sure Aristotle always had what he needed to conduct his scientific studies. He helped Aristotle set up his own school in Athens called the Lyceum. The school acquired a huge library and zoo, and it was here that Aristotle would conduct his most important work.

## Why is Aristotle considered the father of biology?

Aristotle's great strength as a scientist was observation, and he put this strength to good use in studying Earth's animals. He compared their anatomy, studied their habits, and recorded thousands of these observations. In

This engraving, which first appeared in one of Galileo's books, depicts Aristotle, Ptolemy, and Copernicus, three of the greatest astronomers of all time. It is meant to show that each astronomer built on the work of the scientists who came before him.

one of his books, the *History of Animals,* he described more than 500 different species.

Without the use of any scientific tools, Aristotle made many amazing biological discoveries. He was the first to realize that whales and dolphins are mammals, like humans. He discovered that birds and reptiles are anatomically similar. He was the first to detect that embryos have beating hearts. He explained animal migration and extinction. He also recognized that humans are part of the animal kingdom.

*Aristotle had one of the earliest scientific research teams. About 1,000 men roamed Greece and the Asian continent collecting specimens of animal life for him.*

### What was Aristotle's most important scientific contribution?

Aristotle did not simply record his observations. His greatest contribution to biology was the creation of a system of classification. He devised a system of grouping animal species by type that remained the best system for over 2,000 years.

Aristotle's classification divided the animal kingdom into two groups: those with blood and those without blood. This is basically the same as Swedish scientist Carolus Linnaeus's classification of vertebrates and invertebrates devised in 1758 (see page 31 for more on Linnaeus). Aristotle divided his blood animals into fishes, reptiles and amphibians, birds, sea mammals, land animals, and humans. His bloodless classification included the following groups: insects, mollusks, sponges and corals, lobsters and crabs, and octopuses and squid. With a few changes, these correspond to groups in Linnaeus's modern classification system.

*Aristotle particularly liked to study marine animals. One sea urchin is named after him. It is called Aristotle's lantern.*

### What were Aristotle's contributions to astronomy and physics?

None. Aristotle was a brilliant biologist, but almost all his ideas on astronomy and physics were wrong. He believed heavier objects fell faster than lighter ones. He believed all matter was composed of the basic elements of earth, water, air, and fire and the heavens were composed of a transparent fifth element called "ether."

Aristotle also believed Earth was the center of the universe, with the planets and stars revolving around it. He

## A Classic Greek Education

Before Aristotle, a Greek education included reading, writing, music, poetry, and athletics. Older students were also taught politics and citizenship. Teachers called Sophists would travel from city to city and lecture in public squares.

Plato established the first permanent school in Athens with his Academy. Philosophy became an important course for students at the Academy. Aristotle's Lyceum added science to the curriculum and even had a museum on campus with collections of plants, animals, and rocks from around the then-known world.

explained the movements of the planets and stars with different spheres surrounding Earth. The spheres were invisible because they were made up of ether. All the spheres were also connected and moved around Earth like the gears in a watch.

Aristotle's authority as a scientist was so imposing that this view of the universe was accepted as truth for nearly 2,000 years. When the great Polish astronomer Nicolaus Copernicus (see page 115 for more on Copernicus) discovered in the sixteenth century that Aristotle was wrong, he was so shocked that he almost doubted himself rather than the great Aristotle.

### Who was Hippocrates?

Just as Aristotle brought the scientific method to biology, a Greek physician brought science to medicine. He discovered so much about diagnosing illness and treating the sick that he is known as the father of medicine.

Hippocrates was born on the island of Cos in the Aegean Sea around 460 B.C. Both his grandfather and his father were doctor-priests at the local temple dedicated to the Greek god of healing, Asclepius. These priests were called Asclepiads, and the sick would come to them at the temple for treatment for their ailments.

The common belief at the time was that the sick had somehow angered the gods and were being punished. Treatment included purifying baths, dream interpretation, magic plants, and offerings such as food and flowers to the offended gods. Hippocrates was the first physician to believe that disease had earthly causes and earthly cures. He started practicing medicine in a very different way than the powerful Asclepiads.

## Aristotle and the Scientific Method

Aristotle's scientific research followed several consistent steps. It was his version of the **scientific method.** His approach consisted of the following:

1.  He determined the subject matter of the investigation and stated the problem to be solved.

2.  He described traditional solutions to the problem.

3.  He presented his doubts about these solutions.

4.  He presented his own solution, supported by his reasoning and evidence.

5.  He refuted the solutions previously proposed.

The weak part of Aristotle's method is that he relied more on deduction than experiments to prove his ideas. One of the reasons for this was that the scientific tools to conduct experiments had not been invented yet. His powers of observation were so strong, however, that many of his deductions proved to be correct.

As science developed over the centuries, improved scientific tools meant more accurate measurements could be taken. Scientists started using the discoveries of previous experiments to search for more scientific truths. A modern scientific method evolved. It includes the following steps:

1.  Observe—using the senses to learn about an object or event.

2.  Collect data—gathering all pertinent information, like the results of previous experiments.

3.  Ask questions—clarifying exactly what is intended to be learned from the experiment.

4.  Hypothesize—asserting a hypothesis, a conclusion that can be tested with observation.

5.  Experiment—using variables, or different aspects of the experiment that can be changed, to confirm results.

6.  Collect data again—seeing if the results support the hypothesis or not.

7.  Share results—aiding other scientists in their experiments.

### How did Hippocrates change medical diagnosis and treatment?

Treatment from the Asclepiads seemed effective simply because most patients recovered from illness themselves. The Asclepiads also had an excuse for their failures: they said that those who didn't recover had angered the gods too much.

Hippocrates' approach to medicine was scientific. The symptoms of the patient were observed and recorded daily. The condition of the eyes and skin, body temperature, appetite, and urine were examined. He would press his ears against the patient's body and listen to the sounds of the heart and other internal organs. He learned that understanding the exact symptoms could lead to an accurate diagnosis.

Treatment was more difficult. We know now that many common diseases are caused by bacteria and viruses. There was no technology to detect these germs in Hippocrates' time. There were no drugs, anesthesia, or surgical tools. An important part of Hippocratic medicine was prevention. As the true causes of diseases became known, physicians could inform their patients how to avoid illness. This became known as prognosis, from the Greek for "to know beforehand."

*The Persian king Artaxerxes offered Hippocrates his entire fortune if he would stop an epidemic that was wiping out his army. Hippocrates turned him down because Greece was at war with Persia at the time.*

## The Treatment of Athletes

Before Hippocrates' time, the only medical treatment available to most Greeks was the ill-informed efforts of the doctor-priests. However, Greek athletes had received expert care since the first Olympian games were held in 776 B.C. in Olympia, Greece. Athletic trainers were highly respected and paid well for their services.

Males in ancient Greece took pride in physical fitness and athletic skills. Most would attend an outdoor gymnasium daily to work on their fitness. Some would train for the Olympian games that were held every four years. These athletes suffered from the same problems as today's athletes: sore muscles, torn ligaments, broken bones, and so forth. The athletic trainers were very skilled at treating these injuries and speeding recovery.

Hippocrates and his followers did experiment with herbs. If an herb was shown to be effective on a certain disease, the information was shared with other physicians throughout Greece who were starting to follow the Hippocratic approach.

### What Hippocratic ideas remain in practice today?

Even though Hippocrates lived nearly 2,500 years ago, many of his ideas sound very familiar today. He would inquire about the family health history to see if any relatives had suffered from similar diseases. He asked questions about the patient's home to see if his or her environment might be causing the illness. He discovered that diet played an important role in preventing disease.

Hippocrates was the first to understand psychosomatic disease, in which physical illness is caused by emotional stress. He even made suggestions on what we call bedside manner. He said physicians should pay as much attention to the comfort and welfare of the patient as to the disease itself. He found that treatment would have more of an effect on a patient who had faith in his or her physician.

## The Humors

Not all of Hippocrates' ideas were accurate. He believed that illness occurred when body fluids were out of balance. These fluids were called humors and included blood, phlegm, yellow bile, and black bile.

The humors occurred when the four main elements of Greek thought—fire, air, earth, and water—mixed with dryness, dampness, heat, and cold. So, overheating the brain with too much bile resulted in fear and the face would flush. Anxiety would result if the brain was over-cooled with too much phlegm.

This theory led to the practice of bloodletting, where blood was drained from the body of a sick person so that disease would flow out with the blood. Hippocrates correctly made the connection between the brain and emotions, but the idea of humors was disproved centuries later when human anatomy was studied more closely.

## What is the Hippocratic oath?

Hippocrates' contributions to medicine were not just scientific. He wrote extensively on all aspects of medicine and his writings are included in a volume of works known as the Hippocratic Collection. It is not known exactly which of the volumes Hippocrates wrote himself and which his followers wrote. Included in this collection is the **Hippocratic oath,** a code of ethics for physicians. Hippocrates probably did not write the oath, but it was given his name because, in ancient times, students studying in Hippocratic schools took the oath. The Hippocratic oath is still taken today by students graduating from medical school.

Physicians who take the oath promise to help the sick, or at least to do no harm. They promise to keep information about their patients private and to teach their science to all who want to learn. The code also prevents physicians from administering any fatal drugs, even if a patient requests them. Many of these issues are questions the medical world still struggles with today.

## Who was Archimedes?

In 213 B.C., Rome attacked the beautiful Greek city of Syracuse on the island of Sicily. Rome had the greatest army and navy the world had ever known, but they were helpless against the weapons of one old man. The old man was one of the most brilliant scientists of the ancient world.

Archimedes was born in Syracuse about 287 B.C. His father was an astronomer and his family was related to Hiero II, the king of Syracuse. Archimedes was educated at Alexandria, Egypt, the center of learning in the ancient world. At Alexandria, he was taught what most scientists of his day were taught: A true scientist should not be concerned with practical problems. Science was meant to study the order of the universe. Building mechanical gadgets should be the business of engineers and merchants.

When Archimedes returned to Syracuse, he intended to devote his life to studying mathematics and astronomy, but King Hiero made repeated requests of Archimedes to build various mechanical devices, especially weapons to defend Sicily against the invading Romans. He spent much of the rest of his life studying and building machines.

*Archimedes calculated the most accurate value of pi in the ancient world. (Pi is the ratio of the circumference of a circle to its diameter and is used in many mathematical calculations.) His figure was nearly as accurate as that calculated by the most sophisticated computers of today.*

Archimedes' greatest contribution to science was in showing the benefits of applying scientific reasoning to everyday problems. He also proved that great scientific principles could be discovered by studying practical problems.

## What is the Archimedes' screw?

Archimedes' first great mechanical invention was a water pump he invented while still a student in Alexandria. Transporting water from the source was a huge task in the ancient world, particularly for farmers. The Archimedes' screw was so ingenious that it is still used today for irrigation in some countries.

Archimedes used his favorite form—the cylinder—to build his pump. A wooden cylinder was surrounded by thin strips of wood wound around it in the form of a spiral. This screw was placed inside a larger cylinder and sealed. A handle was attached to the screw at the top, and the bottom was placed in the water at an angle.

When the handle on the pump was turned, the screw would rotate and water trapped in the spiral would move upward. When it reached the top, it could be collected or simply emptied into an irrigation ditch. The device was also used to drain excess water from inside ships and thus prevent them from sinking.

## Did Archimedes really once run through the streets of Syracuse naked yelling, "Eureka! Eureka!"?

Legend has it that he once did this because he had discovered a tremendous scientific principle. King Hiero had given a craftsman a certain amount of gold to make him a crown. When the crown was presented to the king, he suspected the craftsman of keeping some of the gold himself and adding silver to the gold in the crown. He asked Archimedes to find out without destroying the crown.

According to the legend, Archimedes decided to take a bath at the public bathhouse and ponder the problem. As he stepped into the tub, water overflowed onto the floor and the brilliant Archimedes realized he had his answer. He leaped out of the tub and ran off to the king to tell him the news, yelling, "*Eureka! Eureka!*" ("I've found it!")

The solution involved water **displacement** and proved that every substance has a certain density. Known as Archimedes' principle, it was the first scientific description of buoyancy. The principle states that an object immersed in a liquid is buoyed or pushed upward, by a force equal to the weight of the liquid displaced by the object.

Archimedes knew that a pound of silver takes up about twice as much space as a pound of gold (or has twice the volume). An equal weight of silver will displace more water than gold because it is larger. So, a crown made from a mixture of silver and gold will displace more water than a crown made of pure gold of the same weight. Archimedes measured the displacement of equal amounts of gold and silver, and then measured the displacement of the crown. It revealed that there was silver in the crown. The craftsman was executed.

### How did Archimedes single-handedly hold off the entire Roman army?

When Rome invaded Syracuse in 213 B.C., Archimedes was 72 years old but his mechanical genius was needed to

## "Give Me a Place to Stand and I Can Move the World"

One of Archimedes' achievements was discovering the mechanics of the lever. He knew a small force at one end of a lever could move a great weight if the pivot (or fulcrum) were in the right spot. "Give me a place to stand and I can move the world," he said. King Hiero asked for a demonstration.

Archimedes had a big cargo ship hauled ashore by a large group of men. The ship was then loaded with cargo and passengers. Archimedes attached a system of pulleys (a lever system using ropes instead of shafts) to the ship and sat on shore some distance away. He made a slight turn of the handle attached to the pulleys, and the large ship was lifted toward him on shore.

This woodcut from the 1500s shows how Archimedes used mirrors to defend the city of Syracuse in Sicily from the invading Romans in 213 B.C.

*Archimedes' weapons repelled the Roman army for three years, but Syracuse did eventually fall. Even though the Roman general had given orders not to harm him, Archimedes was killed in the siege.*

save the city. The weapons he invented to defend the island from the Roman invasion were amazing.

He used his knowledge of levers to design catapults—devices that hurled spears and stones with force over great distances toward an enemy—larger and more deadly than any built before. The catapults could hurl immense stones at the ships and sink them with a single blow. Ancient writers said Archimedes also had huge curved mirrors set up on the walls of the city. As the Roman ships approached, the mirrors were positioned to reflect and focus the Sun's rays directly onto the sails. According to the writers, the sails would burst into flames and the ships would sink, but this story may be more legendary than factual.

Archimedes' most frightening weapons of all were probably the huge claw-shaped beams that jutted out from the city's walls. These "claws" were supported by so much counterweight on the interior side of the walls that they could be used to pick up the ships and drop them onto the cliffs and rocks near shore. Many Romans began to think there was a supernatural force behind the walls of Syracuse.

## Who was Ptolemy?

He was one of the most influential astronomers who ever lived. His theories on the movements of the planets and stars, called the Ptolemaic system, stood unquestioned for 1,400 years. The Arab world of the Middle Ages admired his book on astronomy so much that they renamed it the *Almagest,* Arabic for "the greatest." Unfortunately, almost all his astronomical theories were wrong.

Ptolemy was born around A.D. 100 in a Greek settlement in Egypt under Roman rule. This mixture of heritage was common at that time because the Roman Empire dominated both the Greek and the Egyptian civilizations. It is also assumed that Ptolemy spent most of his life in Alexandria because he conducted most of his studies at the great university there. Very little is known of his personal life.

## What is in Ptolemy's *Almagest*?

The *Almagest* was Ptolemy's first and most ambitious work. It is a 13-volume set of books that attempted to include all the astronomical knowledge available at the time. Its main goal was to allow people to calculate the positions of all celestial bodies—the Sun, the Moon, planets, and stars—for any time.

What is most admirable about the *Almagest* is that it gathered in one work all knowledge of mathematics and astronomy available at Ptolemy's time. He added to this history his own studies and theories. It is the first complete book on astronomy that is still in existence.

The *Almagest*'s other strength is that its system for predicting future planetary positions was very accurate. Ptolemy had researched astronomical records taken as far back as 721 B.C. in Babylon. He relied heavily on the records of the famous Greek astronomer Hipparchus, who observed the stars and planets daily from 147 to 127 B.C.

*The Greek astronomer Aristarchus proposed around 270 B.C. that Earth was a planet orbiting the Sun. Scholars rejected this idea as ridiculous.*

This illustration decorated a 1496 Latin translation of Ptolemy's 13-volume *Algamest*, the standard astronomical reference for more than 1,000 years. Ptolemy is shown wearing a crown, sitting to the left of the table below an armillary sphere, an astronomical instrument. The Latin translator, Regiomontanus, is seated on the right.

Ptolemy also personally observed their movements from A.D. 125 to 141.

### What was the Ptolemaic system?

The Ptolemaic system was a series of theories proposed by Ptolemy to explain the order and movements of the universe. Because Ptolemy's system of predicting planetary movement was so accurate, all the theories of the Ptolemaic system became the accepted view for centuries even though many were inaccurate. Ptolemy did realize that Earth was a sphere and not flat, but his system is flawed because it starts with the basic idea that Earth is the center of the universe and the Sun, the Moon, and the planets revolve around the Earth. The idea had been proposed by Aristotle 500 years before and almost all astronomers agreed.

The Ptolemaic system also agreed with the ancient world's idea that the orbits of celestial bodies had to be perfect circles. This created a challenge for Ptolemy, however. It was very clear from his study of the planets'

# The Tools of An Ancient Astronomer

We know of at least three tools Ptolemy used in his calculation of the position of the Sun, the planets, and the stars. To measure the Sun's position, he probably used a quadrant. A quarter of a circle was ruled on a square board and a special line was attached to make sure it was held vertically. There was a pivoting arm on the board with open sights. This arm was moved against the quadrant to determine the Sun's height above the horizon.

A device called an armillary sphere was used for the planets. The sphere contained a series of circles. These circles corresponded to the ancients' view of the heavens as a series of circles surrounding Earth, each holding the planets as they revolved around Earth. The tool was used to give the planets a celestial latitude and longitude.

Ptolemy actually invented a tool to measure the position of the stars—Ptolemy's rules. A stick was held vertically and a line attached to keep the stick straight. A pivoting arm with open sights was attached to one end. The other end had a pivoting board with movable pegs in it. The pegs could be set at previously measured points to calculate the positions and movements of stars.

movements that their paths wandered around the skies. (The word *planet* means "wanderer" in ancient Greek.) Ptolemy devised a clever theory to explain this wandering movement.

He said the planets actually each had two orbits. The first was its perfect-circle orbit around Earth, called its deferent. While the planet was completing this orbit, it was also orbiting around a fixed point on the deferent. This smaller orbit, called the epicycle, explained why the planets seemed to wander. Ptolemy even worked out very complicated mathematical formulas that seemed to support this theory.

The Ptolemaic system also rejected the idea that Earth rotates on it axis. Ptolemy said if this were true, objects thrown into the air would be left behind as Earth spun away from it. It wasn't until Copernicus's work around 1540 (see page 115 for more on Copernicus) that the Ptolemaic system was even questioned and another 150 years after that before people could admit Earth was not the center of the universe.

## What were Ptolemy's contributions to geography?

Ptolemy might rather be remembered for his contributions to geography than to astronomy. His maps of the world were so accurate for the time that they were used by scholars all over the world for centuries. Christopher Columbus based his theory of finding a westward route to India on Ptolemy's maps. Ptolemy's book *Guide to Geography* is often considered the beginning of the modern science of cartography, or mapmaking.

The strength of the *Guide to Geography* is that in it, Ptolemy used the important system of latitude and longitude, the lines on a map that pinpoint certain locations, for the first time. The basic idea of latitude and longitude had been suggested by the Greek astronomer and geographer Eratosthenes 400 years before, but it was Ptolemy who developed a system detailed enough to be practical. The book lists the latitude and longitude of about 8,000 geographical locations known to the ancient world.

Considering the simple tools and conflicting information Ptolemy had to work with, his maps are remarkably accurate. Yet, one of his errors had a huge effect on world history. Ptolemy disagreed with Eratosthenes' correct estimate of Earth's circumference at 25,000 miles. He

*Ptolemy's maps of the skies included 1,022 stars and 48 constellations. They remained the most commonly used sky maps in Europe and Arabia until the seventeenth century.*

## Astrology

A belief in **astrology** was one of the main reasons the ancient world was curious about the positions of the planets. They thought the planets had a direct effect on the world and that the future, especially natural catastrophes, could be predicted by studying the skies.

Ptolemy wrote a book on astrology in which he explained the different effects planets had on Earth. Venus and Jupiter increased heat and dampness on Earth. Mars was associated with heat and dryness, and Saturn could cool and dry Earth. Mercury's effect depended on how close it was to the Sun and the Moon. The strength of the effect was determined by the exact location of the planet.

accepted another estimate of 18,000 miles, greatly under-estimating the distance over the Atlantic Ocean from Spain to India. This mistake encouraged Columbus to set out on his journey to the New World.

## Who was Galen?

Around A.D. 145 in the Greek city of Pergamum, a father had a dream that his son should become a physician. Dreams were very important to the Greeks of the ancient world because they were thought to be inspired by the gods. The father immediately enrolled his 16-year-old son in Pergamum's medical school. The dream wound up having a huge effect on the history of science because this student became the greatest **anatomist** of the ancient world.

Galen traveled widely, gaining medical knowledge from different parts of the ancient world. He also studied at the great school in Alexandria, before starting his career in Rome as a physician and researcher. He became known as the greatest doctor of the Roman Empire, even becoming the personal physician to the Roman emperor, Marcus Aurelius.

The Greeks had a strong medical tradition starting 600 years before with Hippocrates, who separated religion and superstition from medical practice. Galen studied the great physicians of the centuries before him and added his own findings about anatomy to produce the most complete encyclopedia of medical knowledge of the ancient world. It was so admired that it remained the final authority for the medical profession for over 1,400 years.

*Galen's writings on his medical research include 22 volumes of about 1,000 pages each.*

## How did Galen study anatomy?

In Galen's time, the Roman Empire ruled Greece. Like the Greeks, the Romans did not believe in human dissection. Galen was able to find other ways to answer his questions about human anatomy. He found out all he could from studying the outside of the body. He felt bones and muscles to understand their structure and movement. Galen also dissected thousands of animals, especially Barbary apes.

The title page of one of Galen's books shows scenes from the famous physician's life. This edition of Galen was printed in 1541.

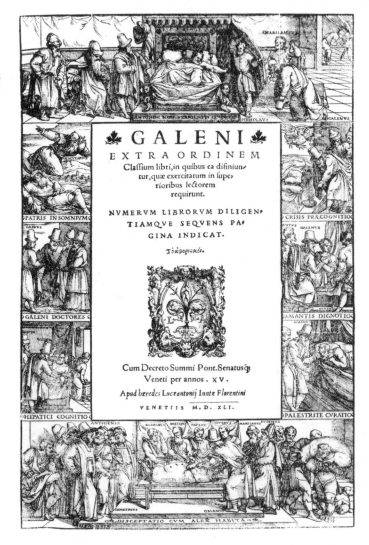

While Galen was in Alexandria, he was able to study the records of two Greek physicians, Herophilus and Erasistratus, who performed the first recorded dissections of the human body around 200 B.C. Egyptian law also did not allow human dissection, but Egyptian rulers had supplied the school at Alexandria with the bodies of some convicts allowing the two physicians to dissect them.

Galen also learned about human anatomy in the gladiator ring. One of his first positions was official doctor to the gladiators in Pergamum. Throughout the Roman

Empire, gladiators fought to the death with swords and other weapons. In treating their broken bones and open wounds, Galen was able to observe many features of human anatomy.

## What did Galen discover about human anatomy?

Galen was particularly interested in blood and its flow throughout the body. He proved that the arteries contained blood, not an airlike substance called "pneuma," as had been believed. His theory was that blood was produced from food intake and that nutrition was supplied to the body from blood flowing in the veins and arteries. Galen identified the muscles, valves, and main blood channels of the heart, but it wasn't until 1628 that blood circulation was truly understood.

Galen also made many discoveries about the nervous system. He learned that all nerves are connected to the brain, many of them through the spinal cord. He cut the spinal cord of animals at different levels and showed which functions were affected. He proved that the larynx and not the heart was responsible for the voice and that speech originates from the brain.

Galen showed that muscles work together. For example, the diaphragm and thorax muscles expand the chest to fill the lungs with air. He showed how emotions affected heart rate and health. He hinted at the idea of genetics by studying how children often have traits of their grandparents rather than their parents.

## What was Galen's approach to scientific research?

Galen's own words express his scientific approach best: "I will trust no statements until I have tested them for myself as far as it has been possible for me to put them to the test. So if anyone after me becomes, like me, fond of work and zealous for truth, let him not conclude hastily from two or three cases. Often, he will be enlightened through long experience as I have."

He believed the object of scientific investigation was to observe clearly and not change observations to fit previous theories. He said that "the surest judge of all is experience alone." His approach of experimentation and

*Like most scholars of his day, Galen spoke both Greek and Latin. Latin was the language of government, but Greek was still the language of science.*

## The Paper War

In Galen's time, a strange conflict broke out between the two intellectual centers of the world—Alexandria, Egypt, and Pergamum, Greece. Manuscripts at the time were written on a paper derived from the Egyptian plant papyrus. The Egyptian ruler Ptolemy (not related to the scientist of the same name) tried to sabotage Pergamum by forbidding the export of papyrus to the Greek city.

Pergamum had to invent a new kind of paper. Scribes started writing Pergamum's manuscripts on a material made from animal skins called parchment. As a result of this invention, Pergamum's manuscripts appeared in the form of a book, similar to what we use today, rather than a roll like the Egyptian papyrus manuscripts. Pergamum won the battle, and parchment eventually replaced papyrus as the paper of choice for manuscripts.

the testing of results is what we today call the scientific method.

Galen was angered by the lack of science in the Roman medical world. He said Roman doctors ignored Hippocrates' teachings and pursued "wealth over virtue." The unquestioning authority his work was given in the centuries after him also would have troubled him. If an anatomical study revealed an error in Galen's work, authorities would say the human body must have changed since his time; Galen could not be wrong. That was not the kind of science to which Galen devoted his life.

### Who was Hypatia?

She was one of the earliest known female scientists and was renowned in her time as an astronomer, mathematician, and philosopher. Scholars came from all over Egypt, Greece, and Rome to hear her lectures, but some despised her for her beliefs. In fact, she was one of the first scientists to die for her beliefs.

Hypatia was born in about A.D. 355 in Alexandria. Though the Egyptian city was nearly 700 years old and showed the scars of several civil wars and fires, it was still the intellectual center of the world. Hypatia's father was Theon, a mathematician and astronomer who taught at

Alexandria's museum. He also taught his daughter these subjects and prepared her for a life as a scientist. Unfortunately, it was a life cut short by ignorance and religious fanaticism.

## What was a woman's usual role in the ancient world?

It was very unusual in the ancient world for a woman to receive the kind of education Hypatia received. It was even more unusual for a woman to become the equal of the greatest minds of the time as Hypatia did.

Women had not been totally excluded from having scientific lives in ancient times. The first recorded reference to a female scientist was in 2354 B.C. in Babylon. A priestess named En'hedu Anna created observatories inside religious temples to map the movements of the stars. She also created one of the first calendars.

In the sixth century B.C., Pythagoras had allowed women into his community of mathematicians and

## The History of Alexandria

Alexandria was built in 332 B.C. by the Greek conqueror Alexander the Great as a center for learning. For 900 years, scholars came to Alexandria to hear lectures from the greatest minds in the ancient world and to study in the huge library. The lighthouse of Pharos, one of the seven wonders of the ancient world, guarded the harbor. Its marble buildings were meeting places where the ideas of cultures from around the world were discussed.

Alexandria's rulers wanted to own a copy of "every book in the world." This often meant stealing books from other cultures and from ships docked in the harbor. At one point, the collection reached 500,000 books.

Around A.D. 385, Alexandria became the center of a bitter religious struggle. Theophilus, a Christian bishop, destroyed the temple of Sarapis. Sarapis was a blend of Greek and Roman gods that had been created to unite the city in a common religion. Theophilus also destroyed a large section of the library for its heathen scrolls.

Alexandria would never be the same. It managed to survive until A.D. 642, when an Arabian army captured the city and destroyed the entire library. Much of the knowledge of the ancient world was lost with it.

philosophers. Hippocrates appreciated the knowledge many Greek women had of herbal remedies, and there were female physicians in the Roman Empire. Aristotle, however, stated flatly that women were inferior to men, so Hypatia's rise to prominence was very unusual.

## What were Hypatia's contributions to science?

In Hypatia's time, it was common for scientists to share their knowledge by writing commentaries, or new versions of old books. By the fourth century A.D., many of the books in the Alexandria library were aging. For example, Ptolemy's *Almagest* was over 200 years old. New copies of these manuscripts had to be copied by hand.

Scholars often took on the job of writing these commentaries so that they could make corrections and add their own findings. Hypatia added her knowledge to several commentaries, including Ptolemy's *Almagest* and Euclid's *Elements*. She is also known to have written original works on astronomy, geometry, and algebra. Unfortunately, all of her original writings have been lost.

*Much of what we know about Hypatia comes from the many letters her students wrote to her long after they were no longer her students. None of her return letters, however, have ever been found.*

A nineteenth-century artist's reconstruction of the world-famous library at Alexandria as it looked during the fourth century A.D.

Hypatia was a brilliant teacher, often giving lectures in her home rather than at the school in Alexandria. She even had mechanical skills and knew how to make scientific instruments of the time, including an astrolabe. (An **astrolabe** was an important astronomical tool used to measure the altitude of stars above the horizon.) Hypatia's students respected her very much and formed lifelong friendships with her.

### How did Hypatia die?

Hypatia also taught philosophy and became the leader of the Neoplatonist movement in Alexandria. Neoplatonism was based on the teachings of the fifth-century

## The Dark Ages

Hypatia's murder was an omen of what was coming. In A.D. 476, Rome fell to barbarian tribes and the Dark Ages began. The Dark Ages were the period in Europe from the 400s to the 900s, when very little scientific discovery took place. There were several reasons why this happened. There was no longer a strong prosperous civilization like Greece or Rome to create a secure society. As Christianity became the most popular religion in Europe, most scholars became more interested in theology, the study of God, than science, the study of nature. Fortunately, some of these religious scholars preserved the ancient works of the Greek and Roman scientists.

During this same time, Arabic scientists were carrying on the scientific tradition of the ancient world and making some discoveries of their own. They made advances in medicine, but they did not use the experimental methods that would eventually lead to the development of modern science. Their greatest contribution was probably the introduction of the Arabic number system into Europe. This system used only 10 different numbers to express all possible measurements. Ease of measurement would lead to a rebirth of science.

Starting in the 1100s and 1200s, scholars like Peter Abelard and Thomas Aquinas started proposing ways to combine Christian beliefs with the scientific ideas of the ancient world. Universities were established throughout Europe. The world of learning, especially science, was about to undergo a rebirth of knowledge and discovery. It was called the Renaissance.

B.C. Greek philosopher Plato. Followers of Neoplatonism believed in the perfection of the human soul through virtue, love of beauty, and intellectual pursuits. They also believed in the existence of a reality beyond man's comprehension. Many scientists and other scholars believed in Neoplatonism because of its emphasis on the intellect, but it was looked upon as a terrible threat by others.

Alexandria was a place of tremendous political and religious turmoil in Hypatia's time as different religious groups fought for power. A Christian bishop came to power in A.D. 385 and took over pagan, or non-Christian, temples for the church. Statues of pagan gods were destroyed, and religious scrolls from the Alexandria library were burned.

In A.D. 412, Cyril became the new Christian bishop and he wanted even more power for the church. The local Roman governor, Orestes, tried to oppose Cyril and had the support of Hypatia, a very influential figure in the city. Cyril accused Hypatia of witchcraft and black magic. He said she even had satanic powers. One night in A.D. 415, a Christian mob attacked Hypatia and murdered her.

Who was Antoni van Leeuwenhoek? ◆ How did Leeuwenhoek improve the microscope? ◆ What did Leeuwenhoek see with his new microscopes? ◆ What was Leeuwenhoek's beasties? ◆ Who was Carolus Linnaeus? ◆ How did Linnaeus's system of classification work? ◆ How did Linnaeus acquire knowledge of so many different plants? ◆ Did Linnaeus believe in evolution? ◆ Who was Charles Darwin? ◆ What are the theories on the origin of living things before Darwin? ◆ What is natural selection? ◆ What was the public reaction to Darwin's Origin of Species? ◆ Who was Louis Pasteur? ◆ What was Pasteur's germ theory?

# AMAZING BIOLOGISTS

### Who was Antoni van Leeuwenhoek?

His trade was producing fabrics and he was the janitor for his town's city hall. He had no university degrees and did not leave his hometown for the last 70 years of his life. It was not the usual background for a scientist in the seventeenth century's Age of Enlightenment, but this scientist had one skill far beyond all others. It would enable him to make some of the most important discoveries in the history of biology.

Antoni van Leeuwenhoek was born in Delft, Holland, in 1632. At 16, he served as an apprentice to a fabric merchant. At 21, he accepted the job as city hall janitor and set up his own fabric business. He was all ready for a quiet life of business—until 1666, when he read a book that would change his life. It was Robert Hooke's *Micrographia,* detailing Hooke's first discoveries with the recently invented microscope.

Dutch lensmaker Zacharias Janssen had invented the compound microscope (a microscope using more than one lens) around 1590. Hooke experimented with the instrument and was the first scientist to use the term "cells," which he used to describe the small pieces a cork seemed to be made of when viewed under the microscope. However, there were problems building these first microscopes, and the instruments could only magnify

Antoni van Leeuwenhoek used his knowledge of lens grinding to create amazing microscopes that allowed him to view bacteria, which he called "beasties."

objects to about 20 times their natural size. Hooke's book inspired Leeuwenhoek to learn how to grind lenses and make his own microscopes. A new field of biology was about to be born.

### How did Leeuwenhoek improve the microscope?

*Leeuwenhoek used his first microscopes to inspect the quality of his cloth as a fabric merchant.*

Leeuwenhoek made tremendous improvements to the microscope of his time. First, he became an expert lens grinder, even working with lenses only ⅛ inch wide. (Lenses must be ground into a curved surface to bend light rays and produce images of objects.) He then decided to scrap the compound system of lenses. Instead, he used one finely polished lens with a mirror beneath it to reflect light onto the slide, a thin piece of glass that holds the object being viewed. He mounted the lenses in frames of copper, silver, and gold and used two screws on the sides to adjust the focus. He even attached handles to the instrument so that he could carry it around with him.

The results were amazing. His simple microscope created a much clearer image and magnified objects to about 270 times their natural size. In his lifetime, Leeuwenhoek made over 500 lenses. He kept almost all of them for his own work, and he never revealed the "secrets" of his craft. However, it was not Leeuwenhoek's skill as a microscope maker that made him a great scientist. It was what he discovered with his microscopes.

## What did Leeuwenhoek see with his new microscopes?

In 1610, the Italian astronomer Galileo (see page 122 for more on Galileo) turned the telescope toward the skies and opened up a new universe to exploration. Leeuwenhoek did the same with his microscope and a different universe. In a long life of careful observation and recording, he made many discoveries.

Leeuwenhoek studied his own blood and discovered red and white corpuscles. He studied the blood vessels of animals and discovered the tiny **capillaries** (from the Latin for "hair-like") that carry blood from the arteries to the veins. Fifty years before, the great English anatomist William Harvey had discovered that blood flows away from the heart in arteries and back to the heart in veins, but he could not see how blood flowed between them. The capillaries Leewenhoek discovered were that missing link.

Leeuwenhoek studied skin, hair, dust, and insects. In plants, he revealed the complex structure of roots, stems, and leaves. Whatever he saw, he verified with many observations and he described in tremendous detail. He hired an illustrator to prepare accurate drawings of his findings. The people of Delft thought he was a little crazy, but the scientists at the Royal Society in London were fascinated by his work. Over his lifetime, he sent the Society 375 scientific papers on his findings.

## What were Leeuwenhoek's beasties?

In 1683, Leeuwenhoek made his greatest discovery. He called them "beasties." One day, he put a drop of stagnant rainwater under his microscope and saw "dozens of little animals, swimming and wriggling in that tiny drop of

*Leeuwenhoek also called some of the microbes he found "animalcules."*

*The Royal Society in London, England, is a group of scientists whose goal is to encourage scientific research. It was founded in 1660, and over the centuries it has rewarded many scientists for their accomplishments with membership in the Society.*

# Spontaneous Generation

The theory of **spontaneous generation** was widely accepted in Leeuwenhoek's time. This theory asserted that lower forms of life, such as worms or lice, originated from nonliving matter. Leeuwenhoek showed that these creatures developed from tiny eggs. He documented the life cycle of ants and the development of larvae and pupae from eggs.

The debate also raged at the time whether, in human reproduction, it was the egg or the sperm that contained the human life. The old idea was that the female uterus merely served as nourishment for the male sperm that developed into a human being.

In one of his rare errors, Leeuwenhoek believed that human life was contained in the sperm and searched for evidence for years. When he could not find it, he made a very unscientific conclusion. He said human ingenuity would never be able to discover that "great secret."

*Peter, Czar of Russia, and Queen Anne of England both visited Leeuwenhoek wanting to peer through his microscopes. Leeuwenhoek was reluctant to let anyone touch his instruments, but since they were royalty, he allowed it.*

water, wretched beasties, a thousand times smaller than you can see with the naked eye." Leeuwenhoek had discovered bacteria.

Leeuwenhoek conducted more experiments to see where the beasties had come from because he did not think the rain had brought them. After weeks of experiments with water from many different sources, he realized that bacteria and other **microbes** (living things visible only under a microscope) are in the air around us and they fall to Earth on particles of dust.

Leeuwenhoek also found bacteria in human saliva. In a remarkable observation way ahead of its time, he found that drinking hot coffee seemed to kill off some of the bacteria. In experiments with shellfish, Leeuwenhoek saw bacteria destroy living things many times their size, but he did not fully understand the significance of these findings. Neither did his successors—it would be nearly 200 years before French chemist Louis Pasteur (see page 38 for more on Pasteur) convinced the world of the connection between bacteria and disease.

## Who was Carolus Linnaeus?

In Aristotle's times, there were 500 different known kinds of animals. With his scientific love of order, Aristotle created a classification system for all 500. (The term we still use for classification, **taxonomy,** is from the Greek for "a system of arrangement.") His system was effective because it arranged animals from the very simplest to the most complex. Unfortunately, this system was ignored, and by the eighteenth century the classification of animals and plants was a mess. A Swedish botanist would bring order back to taxonomy.

Carolus Linnaeus was born in Rashult, Sweden, in 1707. (His birth name was Carl von Linné, but he became known by the Latinized version of his name because his books were published in Latin.) He came from a family of clergymen, but he had no interest in preaching. Even as a child, his only interest was plants. He would transplant wildflowers from the Swedish countryside to his garden and observe them as they grew.

Carolus Linnaeus, the Swedish developer of the system of taxonomy that scientists still use today.

There was one problem with Linnaeus's love of botany, however. There was no way to earn a living as a botanist in Sweden at the time, so he studied medicine and spent several years as a successful doctor. He even became the personal physician to Sweden's king and queen. In 1741, when the king appointed him a professor of botany at the University of Uppsala, Linnaeus could finally devote his life to botany.

*Linnaeus's first book on classification contained seven pages. His final, tenth edition contained 2,500 pages.*

## How did Linnaeus's system of classification work?

Linnaeus had a much bigger task ahead of him than Aristotle did. By the mid-1700s there were 7,700 known species of plants, 4,400 known species of animals, and still no classification system. It was an age of exploration and more and more plants and animals were being brought into Europe from around the world. Linnaeus said, "Without a system, chaos reigns." Naturalists could not share information because there were no common scientific names for any plants. Linnaeus would bring an end to the chaos with a system that is still used today.

The system started with a brief description of each species, or kind, of plant or animal. Next, he grouped each collection of similar species into a genus. He then gave each specimen two Latin names, one for its genus and one for its species. For example, the house cat and the lion belong to the same genus, *Felis,* but they are different species of cat. The house cat's classification is *Felis domesticus* and the lion is *Felis leo.* Even humans have a classification in this system: *Homo sapiens,* meaning "man that is wise."

*One botanist, Johann Siegesbeck, rejected Linnaeus's plant classification system because it was based mainly on the sexual nature of the plants. Linnaeus reacted by naming a genus of useless European weed Siegesbeckia.*

The two-name system is called **binomial nomenclature** and is similar to how human names like John Smith developed. Linnaeus was not through. He went on to group similar genera (plural for genus) into orders, similar orders into classes, and similar classes into kingdoms. When he was finished, he was able to group all living things into two basic kingdoms: plants and animals.

The system was an immediate hit. Naturalists now had a single language in which they could communicate. Simple two-word names in Latin, a language most scientists already knew, now identified specific species. Use of

## A Very Flexible Classification System

One of the great advantages of Linnaeus's classification system was that it was very easy to make changes or additions to it. He knew future discoveries would alter his system but that his basic outline would remain useful. A French biologist, Georges Cuvier (see page 141 for more on Cuvier), made the first changes to Linnaeus's system around 1800.

Cuvier created another level above Linnaeus's classes called phyla. For example, Linnaeus recognized six different classes of animals—mammals, birds, reptiles, fish, insects, and worms. Cuvier grouped these into the phyla of vertebrates and invertebrates. (A level of family was later added between genus and order.)

The 1800s also brought the study of fossils, remnants of living things from the past. Cuvier realized these creatures must be classified, too, and based their classification on a close study of their skeletal remains. This led to the entire system being based more on internal structures than outward appearances as Linnaeus had done. The system was complete—every living thing, alive or extinct, had a clear and specific identity.

the system spread very quickly through Linnaeus's writings and teaching.

### How did Linnaeus acquire knowledge of so many different plants?

Before Linnaeus became professor of botany at Uppsala, he traveled extensively. He traveled to Holland, England, France, and all over Sweden. On each trip, he carefully studied the new plants he came across and filled his notebooks with his observations.

After he became a professor, he often arranged to have his students sent out on exploratory voyages around the world. The students would bring back huge plant collections for their teacher to study. One of his students was the naturalist for the first around-the-world voyage with Captain James Cook. Another student traveled to the American colonies and brought back North American plants. Another of Linnaeus's students became the first naturalist to visit Japan in over a century.

*In 1762, Linnaeus was elevated to Swedish nobility and changed his name back to Carl von Linné. He was given his own coat of arms bearing his favorite flower, the* **Linnea borealis,** *which was named after him.*

*Linnaeus once tried to build a floral clock based on the way certain flowers opened and closed their petals at particular times of the day.*

Other students traveled to Asia, Africa, South America, and Arabia. They not only brought back thousands of specimens, but also spread the word on Linnaeus's classification system, helping it gain worldwide acceptance very quickly.

## Did Linnaeus believe in evolution?

Charles Darwin (see page 35 for more on Darwin) proposed his theory of evolution in 1859, more than 100 years after Linnaeus published his classification system. Its basic idea was **natural selection,** the process by which species changed over many years in order to survive in their environment. These changes led to new species, each specializing in a different way. In evolution, it was called "**survival of the fittest.**"

The theory created an uproar because it challenged many religious beliefs held at the time. One hundred years before, Linnaeus seems to have struggled with the same ideas. His careful studies revealed to him that plants produced hybrids, forms that looked like new species. He saw it clearly when he observed plants from other parts of the world change when they grew in his native Sweden. He could not deny that new species had evolved since the creation of the world. He also called nature a "war of all against all," an idea very similar to evolution's "survival of the fittest."

Linnaeus did not want to be a preacher, but he was strongly influenced by the religious atmosphere of his family. He believed that God had created the world in a divine order from the simplest creatures up to human beings. Linnaeus's need to create a classification system was almost as much religious as it was scientific. Like many scientists of the time, he reached a compromise between his scientific observations and his religious beliefs in what was called a natural theology. He said God created struggle and competition to maintain the balance of nature; it was part of the divine order.

There's no doubt, however, that Darwin was highly influenced by the information Linnaeus so clearly presented in his classification system. Linnaeus did not propose the theory of evolution, but he had planted the seeds for its development.

## Who was Charles Darwin?

The young Englishman came from a family of wealth. Both his grandfather and father were successful physicians. He was supposed to follow in their footsteps, but the first time he saw surgery being performed, he had to leave the room. At 22, he received a theological degree but soon announced he had no intention of becoming a minister. He had another offer. He was to be the naturalist for the HMS *Beagle* as it sailed around the world for five years surveying coastlines. His findings would be the most important in the history of biology, and they would create a religious debate that still goes on today.

Charles Robert Darwin was born in 1809 in Shrewsbury, England. His interest in biology was partly due to his famous grandfather, Erasmus Darwin, who was a well-known naturalist as well as a physician. Darwin's duty on board the *Beagle* was to collect plants, rocks, insects, animals, and fossils and ship them back home for future study.

The young Darwin was having the adventure of a lifetime and was fascinated by the strange forms of plant and animal life he found. The most fascinating stop was the Galápagos Islands off the western shores of South

This photograph of Charles Darwin was taken by well-known Victorian photographer Julia Margaret Cameron in 1868. Darwin's theory of evolution made him a famous—and controversial—figure.

America. Here he saw in the animal life clear evidence that species had undergone slight changes to adapt to the differing environments of the islands. This was the beginning of his theory of evolution, a theory much of the world was not ready for.

## What were the theories on the origin of living things before Darwin?

In Darwin's time, most people still believed in the theory of special creation. This theory stated that Earth and all its living things had been created a few thousand years before and that everything had remained in its original form. Nothing had changed since the moment of creation. Many religions were based on this belief.

Some scientists disagreed. Two Scottish geologists, James Hutton (see page 146 for more on Hutton) in 1785 and Charles Lyell (see page 146 for more on Lyell) in 1830, theorized that Earth was actually many millions of years old. This opened the door for biologists like Jean-Baptiste de Lamarck of France to suggest that millions of years was plenty of time for animals and plants to evolve into new species.

Lamarck was the first to try to explain, in 1809, how this evolution took place with his concept of "inheritance of acquired characteristics." He thought that if a living thing's body changed during its lifetime, then the change would be passed on to its offspring. This proved to be wrong, but it shows that evolution was a scientific issue before Darwin. Some trace its origins back to Linnaeus's classification system, when biologists first became aware of the similarities between species.

## What is natural selection?

In 1836, Darwin came home from his trip around the world with crates of specimens and the beginnings of a theory. New species occurred, but how and why did they occur? It was not until two years later that he had his answer, when he read *An Essay on the Principle of Population* by Thomas Malthus. Malthus said that human population always increased faster than its food supply. This set the stage for a struggle for food and survival.

*The biggest flaw in* On The Origin of Species *was Darwin's lack of knowledge of heredity. Austrian botanist Gregor Mendel (see page 43 for more on Mendel) discovered the laws of heredity just six years after Darwin's book was published, but Mendel's work remained undiscovered until 18 years after Darwin's death.*

Starvation, disease, and even war helped control the population.

Darwin applied this idea to animals. All animals give birth to more young than can survive based on the food supply. Some have to die out so that others can survive. Who dies out? To explain evolution, Darwin came up with the idea of natural selection. He said that in any population of animals, there are variations. Some are born with characteristics that will help them survive, such as keen eyesight, longer beaks, or colors that offer camouflage. As these animals survive, they pass on these characteristics to their offspring. Animals that do not have these characteristics die out.

If the environment changes, new characteristics might become necessary to survive. For example, different colors might be the correct camouflage now. Individuals with these new characteristics will be the ones to survive now and pass on these traits. Over many years, later populations may look very different from the original one. If there are enough differences, a new species will be born. Darwin proposed that millions of years of these changes had led to thousands of different species and that process was still going on.

*Darwin addressed the issue of how humans evolved in* The Descent of Man, *a book written 12 years after* On The Origin of Species.

## Survival of the Fittest

Charles Darwin almost waited too long before publishing his theory of evolution in *On the Origin of Species.* Even though he had devised the theory in 1838 and started writing his book in 1844, he was still working on it in 1858.

In 1858, another English naturalist, Alfred Russel Wallace, came up with his version of natural selection. He called it "survival of the fittest." Wallace had also traveled all over the world studying plants and animals and decided that species must change over time. Wallace wrote a paper on his ideas and sent it to the most famous naturalist in the world, Charles Darwin. Darwin was shocked, but he allowed Wallace to share credit with him when he submitted his first paper on evolution to the *Journal of the Linnaean Society* that year. *On the Origin of Species* was published the next year. Wallace went on to have a long, distinguished career as a writer and lecturer.

Darwin did not originate the theory of evolution, but he did propose an idea on how it worked, and he was the first evolutionist to collect and classify a huge amount of evidence in support of the theory.

### What was the public reaction to Darwin's *On the Origin of Species*?

Darwin had formulated his theory of evolution by 1838. In 1858, he still had not written any papers or books on the theory. He was very concerned about public reaction to a theory that disputed the biblical story of creation. He remembered clearly what had happened to Italian scientist Galileo (see page 122 for more on Galileo) under similar circumstances. He once said publishing his idea would be like "confessing a murder."

When he finally published *On the Origin of Species* in 1859, he made a point to leave references to humans and religion out of it, but it didn't work. The book was banned in many places. Leaders of the Christian church were enraged and attacked the notion that man descended from monkeys, something Darwin was careful not to say in the book.

Darwin stayed out of the fight and allowed the famous zoologist Thomas Huxley to lead the debate for him. During one debate at Oxford University, Huxley defended evolution by saying he would rather be descended from a monkey than a bishop of the Church of England. Many scientists came to Darwin's defense, and the debate eventually subsided.

Darwin saw the controversy coming, but he was still hurt by the personal attacks. He once said, "I have never been an atheist. This grand and wondrous universe seems to me the chief argument for the existence of God." Astronomy had changed man's place in the universe; now biology had changed his place on Earth.

### Who was Louis Pasteur?

The medical profession was not always as scientific as it is today. In the early nineteenth century, barbers performed surgery—the red and white poles outside their buildings stood for blood and bandages. In the case of a

*In the 20 years Darwin delayed presenting his theory on evolution, he spent eight years studying barnacles.*

*After Darwin returned from his travels aboard the Beagle, he was in constant ill health. He never traveled outside England again and seldom even left his home.*

dog bite, the village blacksmith was the source of treatment. He would plunge his red-hot iron into the wound.

There were two problems holding back the medical profession at that time. Even though the Dutch inventor Leeuwenhoek had discovered germs under his microscope in the late seventeenth century, no one had yet discovered the connection between germs and disease. The other problem was that the theory of spontaneous generation, which held that microscopic beings formed spontaneously from surrounding matter by some unknown force, was still widely accepted. Germs were clearly not understood, but because of the work of a French chemist, that was about to change.

Louis Pasteur was born in Dôle, France, in 1822. He was a mediocre student, but he loved chemistry. After receiving his doctorate from the École Normale in Paris, he conducted valuable research into the chemical structure of crystals. Pasteur was a great humanitarian, however—he wanted his work to help people. In 1854, he started studying fermentation, the chemical change that turns grapes into wine. His findings would not only save the French wine industry, but would create a new field of biology and save countless lives.

Louis Pasteur, shown in this 1896 painting by Albert Edelfelt, became a hero of France for his work improving the French beer and dairy industries. His scientific discoveries have helped save millions of lives around the world as well.

### What was Pasteur's germ theory?

It was known in Pasteur's time that yeast cells cause fermentation, but it was believed that it was their death and decomposition that caused the necessary chemical reaction. Pasteur had a new theory: fermentation is caused by the action of living cells, not their decomposition. He believed these living things reproduce; they do not simply appear. To prove his theory, Pasteur studied the organisms of many different ferments—wine, vinegar, milk, beer—under his microscope.

The results were conclusive: the microbes could live without air by extracting energy from the organic substance around it. For example, yeast changes the sugar in grapes to alcohol. Microorganisms in milk change the sugar in milk, lactose, into lactic acid, and the milk sours. Pasteur said that germs are everywhere and that the effect they have on our lives is often very dangerous. The science of microbiology was born.

## The Worst Disease of All Time

It is estimated that during the eighteenth century, 60 million Europeans died of smallpox. The dreaded disease had killed many more than that over the centuries, and those who survived were scarred and often blind. An old English folk cure was that anyone who had ever had cowpox, a very mild disease caught from cows, would never get smallpox.

Dr. Edward Jenner believed that desperate times needed desperate measures. In 1796, he decided to test the folk cure. First, he injected cowpox fluid into the arm of a healthy eight-year-old, and the boy soon developed a mild case of cowpox. Next, he injected smallpox fluid into the arm of the boy and another man—a brave volunteer—who had never had cowpox. The man contracted smallpox, but the boy did not.

This was the first successful vaccination, but Jenner did not know why it worked. That discovery would have to wait for Louis Pasteur, nearly 100 years later. Jenner had taken the first step in a long but amazing medical journey. In 1979, smallpox became the first disease conquered by human beings. Worldwide vaccination had wiped it out.

Now that the process of fermentation was understood, it could be controlled. The wine industry asked Pasteur to study why some of their wine spoiled and some did not. Under his microscope, he studied the yeast cells from good wine and bad wine, and found different shapes between the two. He discovered that once the wine is formed, heat is the solution. If wine is heated to about 120°F, all the remaining yeast is killed and the wine will not spoil. The same process was applied to milk to keep it from souring and came to be known as **pasteurization** in his name.

Pasteur also saved France's silk industry by uncovering a parasite that was destroying the silkworms, but he was just beginning. His discovery of the effects of microbes led him to his germ theory of disease: microorganisms also cause disease in animals and humans. These diseases are therefore infectious because the germs can be carried from one person to another. It was in proving his germ theory that Pasteur, more than any other scientist, probably had the most profound effect on human beings.

*One of Pasteur's final achievements was discovering the germ that caused childbed fever. The germ was streptococcus, which we now call strep.*

### What diseases did Pasteur conquer?

Pasteur always liked his scientific studies to be practical and to serve France and humanity. To begin research into his germ theory, he studied anthrax disease in sheep and cholera disease in hens. These diseases were chosen because they were hurting the French meat and poultry industry and they could infect humans as well as animals. Pasteur found the bacteria that were causing each disease in the blood of the infected animals, but what could be done about it? It took a mistake to find the answer.

One day, Pasteur mistakenly injected some of his hens with an old culture of cholera bacteria instead of a fresh one. The hens did not contract cholera. This was not that surprising—the culture had become weak by exposure to the air. He then injected the same hens with deadly fresh culture. The hens again did not contract the disease. The first injection of weak bacteria had protected them from the disease, or made them **immune.** The implications of this discovery were monumental: any infectious disease could be prevented. Pasteur called this type of injection a vaccine, but he still didn't know if it would work on humans.

Pasteur turned his studies to rabies, a painful, fatal disease that infects animals, usually dogs, and the people bitten by those animals. Pasteur could not find the germ responsible for the disease under his microscope, but he made a brilliant deduction. He knew the disease was infectious, so he concluded that it was caused by a "microbe of infinite smallness." He was correct—it took the powerful electron microscopes of the twentieth century to reveal the virus responsible for the disease.

Even though he couldn't see the germ, Pasteur still managed to isolate it in the nerve tissue of infected animals. He created the vaccine and successfully treated many dogs. One day, a mother brought in her son who had been bitten repeatedly by a dog infected with rabies and begged Pasteur for the vaccine. Pasteur knew the vaccine would also work as a treatment because the rabies germs take a long time to reach the nervous system. He did not like the idea of experimenting on a human, but he also knew the boy would die without it. He injected the boy with the vaccine over several days and watched him recover. Modern medicine had begun.

*Whenever Pasteur experimented on animals in his research, he insisted that they be anesthetized, or put to sleep, because he couldn't stand the thought of any living thing suffering.*

## What effect did Pasteur's discoveries have on medicine?

Pasteur's germ theory completely revolutionized medicine. Barbers and blacksmiths no longer performed surgery, and physicians had a whole new way of treating patients. Pasteur made physicians realize that they needed to boil their instruments and steam their bandages to kill infectious germs. He also told them that they needed to wash their hands in hot water in between patients. As doctors started to follow Pasteur's advice, death rates in French hospitals decreased dramatically.

In England, the noted surgeon Joseph Lister read of Pasteur's findings. At the time, half of his patients were dying after surgery. He started to pasteurize surgical incisions with carbolic acid to kill germs. He found that within three years, this **antiseptic,** or germ-free, surgery cut the death rate by two-thirds.

*Twenty-five years before Pasteur, Hungarian physician Ignaz Semmelweis also suspected that doctors were carrying infectious germs on their hands from patient to patient. He tried to get Austrian doctors to disinfect their hands between patients, but they would not listen.*

Vaccinations were quickly developed against common diseases like whooping cough, tetanus, diphtheria, and later on, dreaded polio. As a result, the number of cases of these diseases was dramatically reduced.. Around the world, countries started treating their drinking water and sewer systems. Germ-killing cleansers were developed, and germ carriers like mosquitoes and rats were eliminated as much as possible. Life expectancy rose in all the countries that took these measures.

### Who was Gregor Mendel?

In one way, the science of genetics, the study of how heredity works, is among the oldest sciences. For many centuries, man controlled the mating of domestic plants and animals to produce desired traits. Warriors needed speed in their horses so they would breed the fastest runners. Farmers would breed the strongest oxen to produce stronger offspring.

In another way, it is one of the newest sciences because it wasn't until the late nineteenth century that a scientific method of predicting the offspring of two particular parents was discovered. The man who discovered these laws of heredity probably had the most unusual career of any of the great scientists.

Gregor Johann Mendel was born to peasant parents in Heinzendorf, Austria (now Hynčice, Czech Republic), in 1822. He helped his parents with farming and had the usual simple education of a peasant boy. His father sold his farm to help Mendel get a college education, but he was still not trained for any kind of career. It seemed to Mendel that the only way to avoid his parents' poverty was to enter the nearby monastery at Brünn (now Brno) in 1843.

*Mendel was born Johann Mendel but assumed the name Gregor in honor of Saint Gregory when he entered the monastery in Brünn.*

Mendel led the quiet life of a monk, teaching science to the local students and tending the monastery's botanical garden, until 1851, when the monastery sent him to the University of Vienna for two years to study natural sciences and mathematics. When he returned to the monastery, his gardening hobby had become a scientific curiosity. How did heredity work? Was there a way to predict the results of crossbreeding? In 1856, he started breeding experiments on garden peas. Nine years and 28,000 pea plants later, he had unlocked the secrets of heredity.

Gregor Mendel, shown in an 1862 photograph, worked in obscurity. The importance of his theories of heredity was not recognized until years after his death.

### What experiments did Mendel conduct?

Mendel chose pea plants for his experiments on heredity for several reasons. Pea plants grow quickly, so many generations can easily be studied. They take up little space, so more plants can be studied to verify the findings. They self-pollinate, which creates purebred plants. They also have seven distinct characteristics, including tall or short plant, green or yellow pigmentation, and smooth or wrinkled seed.

Mendel first experimented with the tall/short trait by crossbreeding pure tall plants with pure short plants. All the offspring of this first generation were tall. Mendel decided to call tallness a dominant trait. Mendel then bred these tall offspring to create a second generation, or grandchildren. The results were surprising. There were mostly tall plants but short plants, had reappeared. The ratio was three tall plants to one short plant, or 3:1. Mendel called shortness a recessive trait.

Mendel then bred the tall plants from the first generation. These plants assumed the dominant trait of tallness but still contained what Mendel called the factor (now called gene) for shortness. They were therefore considered **hybrids,** or mixed plants. He found that when these hybrids were bred, half the offspring were hybrids but the rest were equally divided between pure talls and pure shorts. The ratio of these offspring was 1:2:1.

Mendel repeated the experiments on the other six traits and found the same ratios repeated over and over. After seven years and thousands of tests, he felt his statistics revealed a scientific truth: Inheritance occurs according to scientific laws and therefore can be predicted.

## What are Mendel's laws of heredity?

Mendel summarized his findings in three laws now known as Mendel's laws of heredity. The first is called the law of segregation. It states that offspring receive a pair of genes for each inherited trait, one gene from each of its parents. These pairs separate, or segregate, randomly when the offspring's genes are formed. Thus, a parent hands down only one gene of each pair to its offspring.

The second law is called the law of independent assortment. It states that offspring inherit each of its traits independent of other traits because they are sorted separately. (This law was later shown not to always be true, when American geneticist Thomas Hunt Morgan discovered that two or more genes located very closely on a reproductive cell can be inherited together.)

# Mendel Is Rediscovered: A Show of Scientific Honesty

In 1900, an amazing coincidence took place in the scientific world. Three scientists, unknown to each other, had all discovered the laws of heredity simultaneously. They were Hugo de Vries of Holland, Carl Torrens of Germany, and Erich Tschermak of Austria-Hungary.

Before announcing their great discovery to the world, they checked the earlier work of scientists in the field in various science journals. They all saw a copy of the 1865 journal of the obscure Brünn Natural History Society with Mendel's paper in it. They tried contacting this unknown scientist and discovered he had died 16 years before. Instead of taking credit for the discovery, each man admitted that credit for the laws of heredity truly belonged to Gregor Mendel.

The third law is the law of dominance. It states that when offspring inherit two different genes for a trait, one gene will be dominant and the other will be recessive. The trait of the dominant gene will appear in the offspring.

## What was the reaction to Mendel's findings?

Mendel knew he had made a great scientific discovery. He wrote a paper on his findings and presented it to the Brünn Natural History Society. They either didn't know what he was talking about or didn't understand the significance of it. The paper, *Experiments with Plant Hybrids,* was also published in the society's small scientific magazine, but again there was no reaction. Mendel sent the paper to scientists throughout Europe, but they were not interested in the work of an amateur and a monk.

Mendel was appointed abbot of the monastery soon after that and spent the remaining 15 years of his life running the establishment. His new responsibilities and the disappointing reaction to his work meant there would be no more research. When he died, his laws of heredity were still unknown. It was not until 1900 that three scientists working on heredity discovered Mendel's paper and revealed his findings to the world.

## Who was George Washington Carver?

He was born into slavery during the American Civil War. From the age of 12, he roamed the country alone trying to get the education his bright mind needed so badly. He overcame many obstacles and became the first African American to receive a graduate degree in agriculture. His talents in botany would save the economy of the South, the region that had once enslaved him.

George Washington Carver was born near Diamond Grove, Missouri, in 1864. When he was a baby, Carver and his mother were kidnapped by a Confederate gang called bushwhackers. He was returned to his owners, but he never saw his mother again. Carver's father was also dead, so his owners, Moses and Susan Carver, raised George and his brother as free men.

After he left the Carver farm at age 12, Carver roamed through Missouri, Kansas, and Iowa for 14 years. He set-

*In the early 1900s, Swedish scientist Nilsson Ehle used Mendel's findings to create a strain of wheat that would easily grow in Sweden's cold climate.*

tled in Kansas long enough to finish high school, but getting into college was a problem. Very few colleges admitted African Americans at the time, so Carver worked at menial jobs doing laundry, housekeeping, or gardening just to survive. At the age of 27, he was finally admitted to Iowa State University, which had one of the leading agricultural schools in the country.

After receiving his graduate degree from Iowa State, Carver became a teacher for Tuskegee Institute in Alabama. The college had been founded by Booker T. Washington to help educate African Americans in the South. When Carver arrived at the college, he found the equipment for his agricultural department consisted of one ax, one hoe, and a blind horse. Despite the school's shortcomings, Carver would spend the next 47 years at Tuskegee making some of the most amazing breakthroughs in agricultural science the country had ever seen.

George Washington Carver is here shown teaching his students methods of soil analysis some time in the late 1800s. Carver taught Southern farmers about crop rotation, which aided their production and boosted the economy of the South.

### What is crop rotation?

In the early 1700s, Charles Townshend started experimenting with crop rotation in England. At that time, farmers usually grew the same crop on the same land year after year. Eventually, the crop started to grow so poorly that farmers had to leave one or two of their fields fallow, or unused, for full growing seasons. Then, Townshend found that he could use all his farmland all the time if he changed crops and grew turnips in one of his four fields.

He grew grains in at least two other fields and found that each crop had a different effect on soil nutrients. Different crops added different nutrients to the soil and they absorbed different nutrients from the soil. This was a tremendous improvement on the previous system. By the late 1700s, Townshend's system caught on and English farmland was much more productive and healthy.

When Carver got to Tuskegee in 1896, the South was experiencing a big problem with its farmland—the soil was worn out. For generations, farmers had only grown cotton or tobacco, both of which deplete the soil of nutrients, especially nitrogen. Carter advised southern farmers to start a crop rotation system of cotton or tobacco part of the time and legumes like peanuts the rest of the time. Legumes are plants that produce nitrogen and add it back to the soil.

*On Friday nights at Tuskegee, Carver drove a mule-drawn wagon filled with farming equipment and seeds into the countryside. He taught black farmers about new farming methods and nutritious diets.*

Black and white farmers alike started to use the system, and the economy of the South was transformed. By the 1920s, the peanut was one of the South's leading crops. In fact, Carver's system was almost too successful. Farmers found their soil improving and their crops plentiful, but they also had a large surplus of peanuts. They needed Carver's help again.

### Did Carver really find over 300 uses for peanuts?

Yes, and some have become important parts of our lives. He started with different foods he could make from the peanut and made peanut oil and peanut butter. He also found that flour, molasses, cheese, and milk could be made from peanuts.

Carver combined his biology and chemistry skills by separating the different parts of the peanut—its starches, amino acids, and oils—and recombining them into many nonfood products. He made dye, soap, ink, and rubber from peanuts. He even found uses for the peanut shells in insulating boards for building and fuel briquettes. Carver could have become very rich from all his discoveries, but he chose to patent almost none of them. He wanted to make it easier for everyone to share in their benefits.

Congress was so impressed with Carver's accomplishments that they passed a law imposing a tax on imported

## More Crops, More Products

Carver's botanical studies were not limited to the peanut. He discovered that other plants renourished the soil and had many uses. He found over 100 products that could be made from the sweet potato, including molasses, paste, and rubber. He created a process to obtain paint pigments from clay. This was another economic boost for the South because the region had huge clay deposits. After researching the pecan, he made a material from it that could be used for paving highways. Carver also introduced a legume from China into American farming: the soybean.

peanuts to support America's peanut industry. Carver received many honors as a result of his research, but he could not escape the segregation laws of the South. When he was invited to speak to the newly formed United Peanut Growers Association in Montgomery, Alabama, he still had to enter the building by the rear door.

### Was Carver America's first environmentalist?

Carver had many thoughts on the environment that were years ahead of their time. He once said, "There is no better plant food than the things we ignore or throw away every day." He taught his students how to make compost of leaves, garbage, and weeds long before the organic gardening movement of the late twentieth century.

*The inventor Thomas Edison once offered Carver a position in his research laboratory. Carver turned him down.*

He believed that all things in the world are interconnected and that to ignore this fact can have disastrous effects. He said all our actions on our environment "must be considered in the light of its overall, long-term consequences, not just its immediate benefits."

Carver seemed to foresee the "reduce, reuse, recycle" approach of the conservation movement. He said, "Waste is man-made. Nature produces no waste; whatever is consumed is returned to the whole in a reusable form. Man fails to utilize appropriately the bounty of nature."

### Who are James Watson and Francis Crick?

Even though his work lay undiscovered for over 30 years, Gregor Mendel uncovered the basic secrets of genetics. His laws revealed that genes were responsible for inheritance, but what were they made of and how did they work?

After 1900, huge advances were made in the power of microscopes. Scientists could now see inside the cell. They discovered that cells contain a nucleus surrounded by a protective membrane. Inside the nucleus are **chromosomes,** threadlike structures that contain chemical information about how cells are to develop as the organism grows. Inside the chromosomes, scientists discovered a chemical they called DNA (deoxyribonucleic acid). DNA contained the genes, but to understand how inheritance works, scientists had to determine the chemical structure of DNA.

The discovery of DNA's structure became a scientific race. Among the contestants were two scientists working together at Cambridge University in England.

James Dewey Watson was born in Chicago, Illinois, in 1928. He was a brilliant student and graduated from the University of Chicago at the age of 19. After he heard a lecture by Maurice Wilkins, another scientist working on DNA, he decided to join the DNA research team at Cambridge. He was only 23 years old.

Francis Harry Compton Crick was born in Northampton, England, in 1916. He received his university degree in physics in 1937, but he had been studying cellular structure for several years when Watson arrived at Cambridge in 1951. Together they would make one of the greatest scientific breakthroughs of all time.

## How did Watson and Crick determine the structure of DNA?

Watson and Crick started with the work of American scientist Linus Pauling, another contestant in the DNA race. Pauling had already determined that many proteins, one of the main components of cells, had the structure of a helix, a spiral chain in the shape of a twisted ladder. Watson and Crick decided to start with a helix shape, but how many chains were there?

They next looked at the existing X-ray photos of crystalline DNA that had been taken by British chemist Rosalind Franklin for Wilkins. Wilkins had studied the photos and thought DNA had two chains, or a double-helix structure, but he chose not to research it further. Watson and Crick agreed with the two-chain theory, but their work was just beginning.

Previous research had also revealed that DNA was made up of compounds called **nucleotides.** Nucleotides were composed of sugar, phosphate, hydrogen, and one of four bases—adenine, guanine, thymine, or cytosine. It was also known that DNA contained an equal number of adenine and thymine bases and an equal number of guanine and cytosine bases. With this information, Watson and Crick made a vital conclusion: DNA must form replicas of itself just like chromosomes do during cell division.

Watson and Crick created their double-helix model with each rung of the twisted ladder consisting of one of the two pairs of bases held together by the hydrogen atoms. When the DNA ladder divides at the middle of each rung, the legs form two new ladders because the same two bases always join to make a new rung.

The model not only made sense of all the previous information that had been gathered about DNA, but also explained how genetic information is passed on from generation to generation. The order in which the atoms are arranged makes the code by which information is passed on. The DNA code, which Leeuwenhoek had once called the "great secret," had been uncovered.

## Why was the discovery of the structure of DNA so important?

Three years after Watson and Crick proposed their model, American scientist Arthur Kornberg proved its accuracy by producing a molecule of DNA. Other research showed that the exact sequence of the chemical rungs of the DNA ladder determines the identity of the living organism. Even Watson and Crick, however, probably could not have predicted the eventual consequences of their discovery.

Using DNA, scientists can now make new forms of DNA using genetic material from two different organisms. The process, called genetic engineering, has already been used to produce huge amounts of human insulin for

*DNA is now used in court to prove the innocence or guilt of those accused of crimes because each individual's DNA is unique like a fingerprint.*

*If stretched out, a single strand of human DNA would be 3 feet long and contain 6 billion "steps" of information.*

diabetics. The process has been used in agriculture to improve crops. Genes for specific diseases like cancer have been identified, and the eventual cures for these diseases probably will entail manipulation of these genes.

Watson himself started the Human Genome Project in 1988. The goal of the project was to determine the exact location, chemical composition, and function of all human genes. The gene map or genome, was completed in 2000, several years ahead of schedule because humans have far fewer genes—only about 30,000—than originally suspected. The genome will now be studied to discover tests and possible cures for thousands of hereditary diseases.

The possibilities seem endless. Will we bring extinct species back to life by engineering their genes found in fossils? Will we create brand-new species by combining the genes of two different organisms? Will we create superhumans by eliminating so-called bad genes? Scientists have reached the point where they need to ask themselves, "How far do we want to go?"

### Who was Rosalind Franklin?

In 1962, Watson, Crick, and Wilkins won the Nobel Prize for physiology. Since then, the contributions of a women scientist to the discovery of the DNA model have been a source of great controversy. She produced the first usable X rays of DNA ever taken. Watson and Crick used her pictures to devise their DNA model. Unfortunately, only living people are awarded Nobel Prizes, and she died in 1958. Was she treated unfairly?

Rosalind Franklin was born in London, England, in 1920. From an early age she was interested in science, especially astronomy, chemistry, and physics. She received her doctorate from Cambridge University in 1945 and then studied a special kind of X-ray photography called X-ray crystallography.

*Linus Pauling had already won two Nobel Prizes when the DNA structure race began. He won the Nobel Prize for chemistry in 1954 and the Nobel Peace Prize in 1962 for working to end nuclear weapons testing.*

She became such an expert at this kind of X ray that she was asked to take part in the DNA research team at Cambridge. Tremendous disagreements arose between her and Wilkins and Watson. Her photos had become clear enough to suggest an X shape, but Franklin did not want to commit to a double-helix shape until she had proof.

Rosalind Franklin was the first researcher to produce useable X rays of DNA.

The pressure at Cambridge to win the DNA race led to Franklin's data being given to Watson and Crick without her permission. Franklin's work was the final piece they needed to solve the DNA puzzle. However, she was not mentioned in their first paper announcing the discovery. She spent the last few years of her life studying viruses and how they cause human disease. She died in 1958 at the age of 37.

## Taking Pictures of Atoms

Rosalind Franklin's contribution to the discovery of DNA structure was her photos of the molecule taken with X-ray crystallography. The process had been developed by two British physicists, William Henry Bragg and his son, William Lawrence Bragg. The son would later become head of the DNA research team at Cambridge University.

In X-ray crystallography, X-ray beams are sent through a crystal of a substance such as a fiber of DNA. When the X rays strike the atoms in the crystal, they bounce off at an angle and make an image on photographic film. These images reveal how the atoms of the substance are arranged. However, the arrangement is flattened into a two-dimensional picture. In the case of DNA, the three-dimensional model was needed to understand its structure.

## Who were Louis Leakey's "trimates"?

In the mid–twentieth century, British anthropologist Louis Leakey (see page 155 for more on Leakey) discovered ancient fossils of humans and other primates in Africa. The fossils ranged in age from 5 million to 1 million years old. These discoveries gave rise to the science of paleoanthropology, the study of the origin of humans. Leakey believed humans and other primates had a common ancestor millions of years ago. As this ancestor evolved into humans, or *Homo sapiens,* there were four key developments: walking on two legs instead of four; a larger, more complex brain; the making of tools; and language.

In the 1960s, Leakey decided that a study of primate behavior in the wild would be helpful in the research on the origins of humans. Leakey sponsored three ethologists—scientists who study animal behavior—who came to be known as the "trimates." In 1960, Jane Goodall began her study of chimpanzees in Tanzania, Africa. In 1967, Dian Fossey began her study of mountain gorillas in Rwanda, Africa. In 1971, Birute Galdikas began her study of orangutans in Borneo, Indonesia. Leakey was right: their work has led to a greater understanding of human behavior and our place in nature.

## Who was Jane Goodall?

Jane Goodall was born in London, England, in 1934. As a child, she never liked school but she loved to read and, most of all, she loved animals. After graduating high school, she had a chance to visit Africa in 1960 and her life changed forever. On this trip, she met Louis Leakey. Even though Goodall had no training in zoology, Leakey was very impressed with her desire to study animals in the African wild. He obtained funds for Goodall to study the behavior of chimpanzees, humans' closest primate relative.

Goodall set up camp in Gombe National Park in Tanzania, but it took her several months to gain the chimps' trust to enable her to observe their behavior. Her findings surprised the scientific world. She found that chimps are not vegetarians as previously thought. Even more surprisingly, she found that chimps make and use simple tools. For example, they will strip a twig and use it to dig out a meal of termites from a tree stump. They also use stones to break open nuts. Although chimps are very social animals and display affection toward each other, Goodall also saw two chimp communities wage a violent war until one community was wiped out.

Chimpanzees are now an endangered species, and Goodall spends most of her time trying to save them from extinction. The chimps' natural habitats are being destroyed as humans clear forests for farmland. Mother chimps are killed by poachers so that baby chimps can be seized as pets or even for medical research. In 1975, Goodall established the Jane Goodall Institute for Wildlife Research, Education, and Conservation to help educate the public about the importance of the chimpanzees' survival in the wild.

*Chimpanzees communicate with body postures, facial expressions, and hand gestures. They greet other by embracing or by touching different parts of each other's bodies.*

### Who was Dian Fossey?

Dian Fossey was born in San Francisco, California, in 1932. Even though she loved animals and wanted to become a veterinarian, she received a college degree in occupational therapy. She started a career as a therapist, but her mind was still on animals, particularly the rare mountain gorillas of central Africa. In 1963, she went on a seven-week African safari that included a visit with Louis Leakey at his Olduvai Gorge dig site in Tanzania. Goodall's study of chimps was proving very valuable, so Leakey wanted to set up a similar research study of mountain gorillas. After meeting Fossey, he decided she was the woman for the job.

By 1967, Fossey was in the Karisoke Research Center in Rwanda observing mountain gorillas. She discovered that they are not the ferocious predators many believed. To gain acceptance by the gorillas, Fossey imitated their habits and sounds. She found them to be a peaceful species that live in stable family units like humans. They are mainly vegetarians, although they will eat insects also. Fossey found that each family has a dominant male who will fight fiercely to protect all the infants in his group. She also observed group members caring for each other when they were sick or injured.

Like Goodall, Fossey found herself fighting the human activities that threaten the mountain gorillas with

*Since 1972, researchers at Stanford University have taught a sign language to a female gorilla named Koko. Koko has learned hundreds of signs and uses them to communicate with humans.*

extinction. Their habitats are disappearing, and poachers kill many adults for trophies and trap baby gorillas to sell to zoos. Fossey's efforts to protect the mountain gorillas made her an enemy of the poachers. In 1985, she was found murdered in her Karisoke cabin, probably another victim of the poachers.

## Who is Birute Galdikas?

Birute Galdikas was born in Wiesbaden, Germany, in 1946. She also had an interest in animals from an early age and was especially fascinated by orangutans. Along with chimps and gorillas, orangutans are humans' closest living relatives. Galdikas's family moved from Germany to Canada and then to the United States, and Galdikas studied anthropology at UCLA. In 1969, Leakey was giving a lecture at the university when Galdikas asked him to sponsor an orangutan research project for her similar to Goodall's and Fossey's. He agreed, and in 1971, Galdikas found herself in Camp Leakey in Borneo, Indonesia, one of the orangutans' last remaining homes.

Galdikas found the orangutan's behavior quite different from that of chimps and gorillas. The orangutan is not a social animal like the other great apes. They lead solitary lives, except when females are raising their young, and they rarely leave the treetops of their rain forest habitat. They eat mostly fruits and also make use of simple tools like twigs to find insects. Galdikas often witnessed males fighting each other when a female was present. As they fought, their fleshy cheek pads would expand and their loud screams could be heard a mile away.

The orangutan is also an endangered species due to human activities. Their rain forest habitats are quickly disappearing, and poachers kill them and capture their babies for zoos. Galdikas has also discovered that female orangutans in the wild give birth only once every eight years. This extremely low birthrate also threatens the survival of this species in the wild. The work of Galdikas, like that of Goodall and Fossey, is not only important in trying to help our closest relatives survive on Earth. It also gives us a close look at how our ancestors lived millions of years ago.

What was alchemy? ◆ Who was Joseph Priestley? ◆ How
did Priestley make the first soda pop? ◆ Who really
discovered oxygen? ◆ Why was Priestley forced to
leave England and emigrate to America? ◆ Who was
Antoine Lavoisier? ◆ What is the law of the conservation of matter? ◆ What does oxygen have to do with
all this? ◆ What were some of Lavoisier's other discoveries? ◆ What was Lavoisier's horrible end? ◆ Who first
proposed the theory of the atom? ◆ Who was John
Dalton? ◆ How did Dalton's study of meteorology lead
to his atomic theory? ◆ How could Dalton weigh
atoms? ◆ What is Dalton's atomic theory? ◆ Who was

# AMAZING CHEMISTS

## What was alchemy?

Modern chemistry had its beginnings in the strange practices of alchemy. Alchemy got its name from an Arabic word meaning "Egypt" because at first it was a secret cult of Egyptian priests. From their studies, the priests learned glassmaking, metalworking, and methods of preserving mummies. By the time alchemy reached Europe centuries later, alchemists had a single goal: to turn common metals into gold.

Alchemists never succeeded in turning other metals into gold, but they did make some interesting discoveries. The Flemish alchemist Jan van Helmont started to turn alchemy into the science of chemistry around 1630. His experiments produced fumes, or gases, as he called them, and he noticed how different the gases appeared. They were different colors. Some would extinguish flames and some would burn if lit. He concluded that each gas was an airlike substance, but he did not know how to study the gases because they mixed with the air so quickly. An eighteenth-century English minister would solve the problem and become the discoverer of oxygen and soda pop.

## Who was Joseph Priestley?

Joseph Priestley was born in Leeds, England, in 1733. He was raised by an aunt who was a member of a religious group called the Dissenters. The freethinking group rejected many of the beliefs of the Church of England and gave Priestley a spirit of rebellion that would stick with him throughout his life. He studied for the ministry and became a pastor for a small Dissenting church in Leeds in 1766. He might have stayed a country pastor the rest of his life but for a chance meeting with Benjamin Franklin that same year.

Franklin had become world famous for his studies of electricity and his support of the American independence movement. Priestley was interested in both aspects of Franklin's life. The meeting inspired Priestley to conduct some experiments in electricity and write a book called *The History of Electricity*. Priestley's scientific fame, however, would lie in another field—he returned to the ideas of the alchemist Helmont and became one of the founders of modern chemistry.

### How did Priestley make the first soda pop?

Priestley's next-door neighbor in Leeds was a brewery. He became fascinated by the gases that rose out of the beer vats and thought of Helmont's desire to capture

Joseph Priestly, who advanced the knowledge of chemistry immeasurably in the 1700s, also invented the first soda pop.

gases. Some scientists tried to capture gases using a bent pipe and an upside-down water-filled bottle. The gas was supposed to rise up through the pipe and force out the water, leaving a bottle full of gas, but most gases dissolved in the water. Priestley used mercury instead of water and found the gases did not dissolve.

Priestley captured the gas from the brewery and studied it carefully. He found it extinguished a flame and was heavier than air. When he mixed it with water, it made a pleasant, sparkling drink. The gas was carbon dioxide and the drink was the first soda pop. Priestley also produced the gas nitrous oxide and noticed its strange intoxicating effect. Many years later this "laughing gas" would become the first anesthetic used for surgery.

In a brilliant display of curiosity, Priestley placed a plant in a container with some water and covered the container. He then lit a flame in the container until it burned out. Several days later, he was able to light the flame again. He covered the container again and was able to keep a mouse alive in the air provided by the plant. Priestley did not know exactly how it worked, but he had observed respiration—plants taking in carbon dioxide and releasing oxygen.

## Who really discovered oxygen?

In all, Priestley discovered nine gases. He did not know what these gases were, but he isolated them and described their properties. One of these discoveries could have disproven an incorrect theory called the phlogiston theory of fire, but Priestley drew the wrong conclusion from a successful experiment.

The phlogiston theory was developed in the early 1700s by German chemist Georg Ernst Stahl to try to explain fire. He said that all flammable materials contained a substance called **phlogiston** and that materials gave off phlogiston as they burned. Air was needed for fire because it absorbed the phlogiston that was released. Plants removed phlogiston from the air and became filled with the substance, so they would burn easily when dry. Stahl was close except for one thing: there's no such thing as phlogiston.

*Some of the other gases discovered by Priestley include ammonia, carbon monoxide, and sulfur dioxide.*

## Out of Chaos, Gas

The Greeks had a myth to explain the beginning of the universe. They said it started with thin matter without structure that spread out everywhere. They called this original matter "chaos." When the alchemist Jan van Helmont started noticing these airlike substances, he thought that chaos would be a good name for them. However, Helmont spoke Flemish, so when he said "chaos" with a Flemish accent, it came out "gas" and he spelled it as he pronounced it.

*In 1780, Priestley became a member of the Lunar Society, an organization of the leading scientists of the day. They met on nights with full moons to have light for their trips home. They came to be known as the "lunatics."*

Priestley came close, too. In 1774, he conducted the most important experiment of his life. He used his mercury pipe and burned some mercuric oxide (called "calx" at the time), a substance created by heating mercury. The gas that was trapped as a result had an unusual property: a candle inserted into it would burn brightly. Most other gases extinguished flame. He also found that a mouse would live much longer in this gas than in plain air. The gas was oxygen, but Priestley called it "dephlogisticated air." He still believed Stahl's theory.

In 1771, the Swedish chemist Carl Scheele also produced oxygen by heating various compounds, including mercuric oxide. Scheele called the gas "fire air," but his experiments were not published until 1777. Priestley published his findings in 1775, so he is usually given credit as the discoverer, but some science historians give credit to both men. In 1779, the French chemist Antoine Lavoisier (see page 61 for more on Lavoisier) named the gas oxygen and disproved the phlogiston theory.

### Why was Priestley forced to leave England and emigrate to America?

Priestley's upbringing as a Dissenter stuck with him throughout his life. He was a freethinker with bold ideas on science, theology, and politics. Despite his interest in experimental science, he remained a pastor his entire life. He wrote often on religion, including his very controversial *History of Corruptions of Christianity*. In this work, he blasted Roman Catholicism as "the chief repository of error" and rejected many of the beliefs of the Church of England as well. The book made him many enemies in England, and it was officially burned by a public hangman.

Priestley also strongly supported the freedom movements of the American and French Revolutions. Dissenters were deprived of citizenship in England at the time, so many shared the democratic, anti-monarchal views of the two revolutions. Priestley was so vocal in his support for the French Revolution that the French government granted him citizenship. They also made him a member of their National Assembly while England's House of Commons denounced him.

*Priestley invented the pencil eraser when he discovered that a substance called India gum could be used to rub out pencil writing.*

When England and France went to war in 1793, Priestley's position in England became dangerous. His church, home, and laboratory in Birmingham were burned to the ground by an angry mob as Priestley fled to London with his family. He could find no support in London either—even his scientist friends deserted him.

Priestley emigrated to America and spent the final 10 years of his life in Pennsylvania. Leaders of the American Revolution like Franklin, John Adams, and Thomas Jefferson welcomed him as a hero and attended his sermons. Priestley would probably rather be remembered as a theologian than a scientist, but his discoveries made him one of the founders of modern chemistry.

## Who was Antoine Lavoisier?

In 1765, the French government asked a 22-year-old lawyer to make a study of the best way to light the streets of Paris at night. The young man made a close study of fuels and combustion, or burning. He found the best type of oil to burn for the streetlamps, the best time to light the lamps, ways to reuse the oil, and ways to keep the oil from freezing in the winter. His study won him a gold medal from the French Academy of Sciences, but more importantly, it turned a lawyer into a scientist. The scientist would become the father of modern chemistry.

Antoine-Laurent Lavoisier was born in Paris in 1743 to aristocratic parents. His father was a wealthy lawyer and expected his son to follow in his footsteps. Lavoisier received his law degree and was admitted to practice, but

*Lavoisier was put in charge of a French government agency controlling the production of gunpowder. He increased production so much that France was able to supply the American colonies with much of the ammunition needed to defeat the British in the American Revolution.*

even during college he was more interested in science. He took many chemistry courses and even met the great Swedish naturalist Carolus Linnaeus.

His study of lighting and combustion for the government convinced him his future was as a chemist, not a lawyer. However, he still needed a job to support himself while he conducted his scientific research. He used the aristocratic contacts of his family and became *fermier général,* the chief tax collector for the monarchy of France. It was a decision that would eventually lead to one of the most horrible ends of any of the great scientists.

## What is the law of the conservation of matter?

By 1770, Lavoisier was carefully studying how combustion worked. How did things burn and how did they rust? Stahl's phlogiston theory was still accepted, but Lavoisier had a problem with it: the theory had never been proven with measurements. Two hundred years before, Galileo had stressed the importance of measurement in astronomy. Lavoisier wanted to apply that to chemistry.

He started burning many different substances and weighing the results. Wood turned to ash and was much lighter. Candles burned and left nothing behind. He even burned a diamond and watched it seemingly vanish. Where did the disappearing matter go? Tin, sulfur, and phosphorus all seemed to gain weight when burned. Lavoisier then studied rust and found that metals were heavier when they rusted. Where did the extra matter come from?

Even the alchemists knew that burning substances created gases. Lavoisier devised an apparatus with sealed containers where he could capture gases released during combustion and measure their weight. In this way, he could also measure the amount of gas absorbed as a result of rust. He placed a piece of wood in the sealed container and weighed it. Then he burned the wood until it was ash and weighed the container again. This time the weight was the same. He burned tin, sulfur, and phosphorus with no weight change. He allowed a piece of iron to rust in the container and weighed it. Again, the weight did not change.

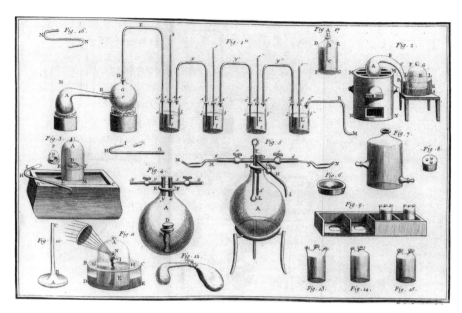

Lavoisier had discovered chemistry's first great law, the law of the conservation of matter. This law states that matter can neither be created nor destroyed; it can only change from one form to another. For example, when wood is burned, the amount of solid weight that is lost when the wood turns to ash is exactly equal to the amount of gas weight added to the air. The law is the basis of all present-day chemical formulas.

French scientist Antoine Lavoisier used these instruments to carefully check changes in weight during chemical experiments. This drawing was made by his wife and assistant, Paulze.

## What does oxygen have to do with all this?

With his new findings, Lavoisier was able to explain how metals were created from ores. The ores were a combination of metal and gas. When the ore was heated, usually with charcoal, the charcoal took the gas from the ore, leaving the pure metal behind.

Lavoisier knew there was another piece of the puzzle missing, though. During his experiments, he saw that not all the gas in the air was being used. It was always only about one-fifth of it. In 1774, Joseph Priestley visited Lavoisier in Paris and told him of his dephlogisticated air. Lavoisier had his answer: air is made up of at least two gases in a one-to-four proportion.

The one-fifth part, which Lavoisier named oxygen (from the Greek for "acid producer" because Lavoisier

# A Classification System for Chemistry

Lavoisier was a great admirer of the Swedish scientist Carolus Linnaeus, who started a classification system for biology. Inspired by Linnaeus, Lavoisier, and three other French chemists set up a new chemical naming system. An exact system of prefixes and suffixes would now clearly describe chemical compounds. For example, carbon *di*oxide contained twice as much oxygen as carbon *mono*xide.

The new system set the stage for chemical equations to express chemical reactions. One example was fermentation = alcohol + acid + oxygen. Later, symbols were added for each element to make the system even easier. In 1789, Lavoisier published a book called *Elementary Treatise on Chemistry,* supplying all his knowledge of chemistry using the new language system. It also contained the first periodic table of the elements. It was the first chemistry textbook.

*When Lavoisier married at 28, his wife Paulze was only 14, but she went on to become his leading research assistant. She translated all the English and Latin scientific papers for him and drew all the illustrations for his books.*

mistakenly thought it was also a part of all acids), was the part of air that was needed for combustion and, as he was to find out later, life itself. Lavoisier named the other four-fifths of air **azote** (from the Greek for "no life") because it did not support combustion or life. Its name was later changed to nitrogen. Lavoisier did not know there were very small amounts of a few other elements in the atmosphere, but he had disproven the phlogiston theory.

### What were some of Lavoisier's other discoveries?

Some of Lavoisier's other discoveries were so far ahead of their time that his fellow scientists had trouble accepting them. He applied what he had learned about combustion and oxygen to the human body. As a result of his experiments, he knew that we take in oxygen through the air and exhale the waste product of carbon dioxide. Adding that to our intake of food as a "fuel" for energy, he realized that the body heat we produce is a result of the combustion of food and oxygen.

In 1766, the English scientist Henry Cavendish had isolated a very light, flammable gas by dropping bits of iron, tin, and zinc into hydrochloric acid. Cavendish thought he had discovered phlogiston. He was also very confused by the puddle of water that resulted when he burned this gas. The brilliant Lavoisier repeated the experiment and knew exactly what it meant. He named the gas hydrogen (from the Greek for "water-producing") and deduced that water must be a combination of the two gases, oxygen and hydrogen.

## What was Lavoisier's horrible end?

Lavoisier was heavily involved in many official duties for the French government. He was the leader of the commission set up to create a new system of weights and measures. The result was the metric system used in most of the world today. Despite his close ties to the government, Lavoisier was a strong supporter of the French Revolution. It did him no good, however. During the revolution's Reign of Terror, he was linked to his old *fermier général* tax-collecting position for the monarchy. In 1794, at the age of 50, he was sentenced to die by the guillotine.

*After the French king was overthrown in 1789, Lavoisier was made president of the Bank of France. He proposed tax reforms and a new economic system that would be fairer for the poor in the country.*

## Who first proposed the theory of the atom?

The Greek philosopher, Democritus was called "the Laughing Philosopher" because he said the purpose of life was "to be cheerful." Around 470 B.C., he proposed a theory that made others laugh at him. Democritus argued that all matter was made up of invisible particles he called atoms (from the Greek for "indivisible") and that the world consisted of an infinite number of atoms moving in an infinite void. He said these atoms were indestructible and differed from each other in size, shape, and position. The identity of each thing in the world came from a different combination of these atoms. He said that the world formed as a random combination of atoms, and that because there are an infinite number of atoms, countless other worlds must exist.

Democritus's ideas were rejected at the time, and he was even suspected of being insane, but his theory of the atom would not go away. In 1660, the Irish scientist Robert Boyle was studying air and noticed that it could be compressed to take up less space. His conclusion was that air was made up of tiny particles with a large amount of space between them, but what were those particles?

## Who was John Dalton?

The theory of the atom would remain unproven until 1803, when an English scientist presented the proof. John Dalton was born in poverty in Eaglesfield, England, in 1766. He was such a genius at mathematics when he was young that the village allowed him to open up his own school at the age of 12. He later became a teacher of mathematics and science at Manchester College, but his first love was meteorology. It was his study of Earth's atmosphere that led to the most important discovery in the history of chemistry, the discovery of the atom.

## How did Dalton's study of meteorology lead to his atomic theory?

Dalton was fascinated by Earth's atmosphere. He called air "elastic fluid" and made his own weather instruments—barometers, thermometers, and rain gauges—to study it. He made daily readings of the air for 57 years and recorded his findings in notebooks. In all, he recorded over 200,000 observations on the weather in these notebooks, the last one on the day he died.

*Dalton was the first scientist to prove that rain is caused by a decrease in temperature, not a change in atmospheric pressure.*

By Dalton's time, scientists knew that the air consisted of oxygen and nitrogen along with very small amounts of carbon dioxide and water vapor. Dalton collected hundreds of samples of air from all over England—from mountaintops, valleys, and cities. He analyzed the samples and found that the composition was the same in every case. He wondered why the heavier gas, carbon dioxide, didn't settle to the lower elevations.

Dalton conducted experiments in which he separated the lighter and heavier gases and placed them in flasks. He then upended the flask with the lighter gas and placed it on top of the flask with the heavier gas so that the openings met. In each case, the heavier gas did not remain on the bottom; the gases mixed very quickly. This led to Dalton's theory of partial pressures. This theory states that the particles of one gas combine easily with the particles of another gas, but the particles of the same gas do not combine easily. Dalton's theory confirmed his belief in the atom, but he wanted more. He wanted to prove the existence of atoms by weighing them.

## How could Dalton weigh atoms?

He couldn't. The technology to do that was still over 100 years in the future, but he could do the next best thing. He could measure their relative atomic weights. First, Dalton turned to the results of past studies.

In 1799, the French chemist Joseph-Louis Proust followed the lead of Antoine Lavoisier and started measuring the weights of chemical compounds. For example, he found that whenever copper, oxygen, and carbon are combined to form copper carbonate, they always combine in the same proportion by weight. The mixture was always five units of copper, four units of oxygen, and one unit of carbon. He tested other compounds and found the same effect. Proust called his discovery the law of definite proportions.

To Dalton, this was another indication of the indivisible particle or atom. To change the ratio, you would have to cut or divide the particles of one of the elements, but this was clearly not possible. Dalton studied other compounds. He found that carbon dioxide was made up of three units of carbon and eight units of oxygen. Carbon monoxide was made up of three units carbon and four units oxygen. He remembered Proust's copper carbonate and the 4:1 ratio of oxygen to carbon. No matter which compounds he tested, the ratios were whole numbers, never fractions. Democritus would have the last laugh, after all.

*Dalton wrote a book on meteorology that included a correct explanation of aurora borealis as a magnetic phenomenon.*

# A Symbol System for Chemistry

John Dalton published his findings on atomic weights and his atomic theory in 1808 in *A New System of Chemical Philosophy*. The book also included a set of symbols for the elements to help explain his findings.

In 1814, Swedish chemist Jöns Berzelius improved on Dalton's findings. He made some of the atomic weights more accurate and supplied the weights for new elements that had been found. He also replaced Dalton's symbols with the initial letter of each element's Latin name. Oxygen became O, hydrogen H, carbon C, and nitrogen N. Water was $H_2O$.

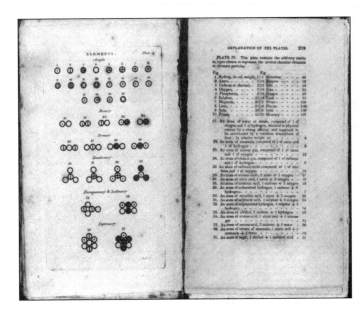

John Dalton developed these chemical symbols in the early 1800s. He used these symbols in a table of atomic weights, which made chemistry a truly quantitative, or measurable, science.

To determine the atomic weights of the elements, Dalton took the lightest element known, hydrogen, and assigned it a weight of 1. He then started weighing compounds like water and found the ratios of the weights of their elements. Simple math gave him the relative atomic weights of the 21 elements that were known at the time. The same formula could be used to determine the atomic weights of any elements discovered in the future—and there were many more to come.

*Dalton was the first scientist to describe color blindness, a disorder from which he suffered. For many years after his study, the disorder was called Daltonism.*

## What is Dalton's atomic theory?

Dalton was now convinced he had enough proof to back up an atomic theory. By 1803 he was lecturing on his theory, and by 1808 he had published his findings. His atomic theory states the following: All matter is made up of small, indivisible particles called atoms. Atoms of different elements have different properties, but all atoms of the same element are identical. The entire atom takes part in chemical reactions. Atoms are not changed when they become part of chemical compounds. Atoms cannot be created or destroyed.

Lavoisier had called for chemistry to become a **quantitative science**—one where careful measurements supported theories. Dalton took a huge step in that direction with his atomic theory. He was immediately lauded by fellow scientists. He was awarded the medal of the Royal Society of England and elected to the French Academy of Sciences. He had unlocked the first secrets of the atom. He could never have imagined the incredible energy that was found in this tiny particle 140 years later with the development of atomic power.

### Who was Amedeo Avogadro?

There are many examples of a scientist's theory being rejected in his lifetime despite its accuracy. Sometimes, fellow scientists want to see a theory proven before they accept it. Pasteur constantly had to prove his theories to his fellow scientists. Often, believers in organized religion feel threatened by findings that oppose their beliefs. Galileo (see page 124 for more on Galileo) and Charles Darwin were criticized for such "heretical" beliefs. Scientists can also feel threatened by contradictory findings, and they might dismiss a new truth rather than abandon an old idea. This is what happened to the discoverer of the molecule.

Amedeo Avogadro was born in Turin, Italy, in 1776. His father was a prominent lawyer and Avogadro planned to follow in his footsteps. By the time he was 20, Avogadro had earned his degree and was practicing law, but he had far more interest in mathematics and science. He began private studies of both, and by 1809 he had learned enough to be appointed a professor of physics at Vercelli College.

Just two years later, Avogadro wrote a paper that explained many of the questions raised by John Dalton's new findings. Avogadro discovered the molecule, a group of atoms joined together that act like a single particle. Like the work of Austrian botanist Gregor Mendel in genetics half a century later, Avogadro's work would be ignored during his lifetime. He died in 1856, an unknown in the science world.

*Avogadro inherited the title of count from his father at the age of 11.*

### What did Dalton get wrong?

Many scientists who make great leaps forward in their discoveries generate as many questions as they answer—like Dalton and his atomic theory. Dalton had proven the existence of the atom, and his relative atomic weights were a brilliant start to measuring the atom, but questions remained. Scientists were still puzzled by the true weight and amount of atoms that made up elements and compounds. In 1814, the Swedish chemist Jöns Berzelius calculated some atomic weights that differed from Dalton's. Other scientists found weights different from those of both men.

Dalton thought that one atom of water was composed of one atom of hydrogen and one atom of oxygen. He also thought that mixing one ounce of hydrogen with eight ounces of oxygen produced nine ounces of water. This would mean one ounce of hydrogen contained as many atoms as eight ounces of oxygen. Scientists started questioning the accuracy of these ideas.

In 1809, the French chemist Joseph-Louis Gay-Lussac found that gases form compounds, like water, in simple, definite proportions of small whole numbers. For example, he found that water actually consists of two parts hydrogen and one part oxygen. Dalton rejected the finding because he still thought that "particles" meant only atoms. He could not see how one particle of oxygen could produce two particles of water, but Gay-Lussac was right and Avogadro knew it.

## What is Avogadro's law?

Avogadro's study of gases and atomic weights led him to two conclusions. First, the atoms of many elements actually occur in groups of two or more, called molecules. A molecule (from the Latin for "mass") is the smallest unit of a substance that has all the chemical properties of that substance. For example, two oxygen atoms bond to form one oxygen molecule, so its symbol is $O_2$. The same is true for hydrogen.

Avogadro then found that "equal volumes of all gases, under the same conditions of temperature and pressure, contain the same number of molecules." This came to be known as Avogadro's law and was the key to determining more accurate atomic weights.

Here's how it works: Take two 1-liter jars under the same temperature and pressure. Fill one with oxygen and

*Avogadro's career as a teacher was constantly disrupted during his life due to the wars and revolution of Italy struggling for independence. The kingdom of Italy was finally proclaimed in 1861.*

# The Number of Molecules in a Substance

After Avogadro's law finally was accepted, some scientists tried to calculate how many molecules might be present in a specific weight of a substance. Eventually, they calculated that 22 liters of gas contains 602 billion trillion molecules.

This is usually written as $6.02 \times 10^{23}$ (to the twenty-third power) and is referred to as Avogadro's number, even though Avogadro had nothing to do with it. It is also referred to as one mole of the substance. To give an idea of its size: If you were able to count atoms at a rate of 10 million a second, it would take you about 2 billion years to count the atoms in one mole.

the other with hydrogen and weigh them. The jar of oxygen weighs 16 times more than the jar of hydrogen. According to Avogadro's law, oxygen molecules then must weigh 16 times more than hydrogen molecules. Since both molecules contain two atoms, oxygen atoms must also weigh 16 times more than hydrogen and therefore have an atomic weight of 16. More accurate atomic weights could be determined using Avogadro's law than with previous methods.

## Who was Stanislao Cannizzaro?

The confusion over atomic weights could have been cleared up decades earlier than it was, but no one was listening. The main reason was that the theory depended on the idea that identical atoms may combine with one another to form a molecule. Chemists at the time could not believe this, so Avogadro lived out the remainder of his life simply as a professor of mathematical physics at the University of Turin.

The confusion over atomic weights continued until 1860, when chemists met in Karlsruhe, Germany, to try to settle the question. At the meeting, the Italian chemist Stanislao Cannizzaro advanced the molecular theory of Avogadro as the clear solution. He had even calculated a new set of atomic weights based on oxygen (16) and Avogadro's law. The argument seemed to fall on deaf ears once again, except for one young German chemist, Julius

Lothar Meyer. Meyer would eventually publish a book, *Modern Theories of Chemistry,* in which he supported Avogadro's molecular theory. Other scientists soon followed, and by 1890 the theory was widely accepted.

## How did the periodic table of the elements develop?

The discoveries of chemists like Dalton, Lavoisier, and Avogadro concerning atoms and atomic weights made it easier for scientists to detect new elements. In 1808, Dalton created a table of the 21 known elements. By 1860 there were 63 known elements and chemists were beginning to notice similarities in the properties of some of the elements. Could a table be constructed that would bring a meaningful order to the elements and reveal a pattern to their properties?

The first serious attempt at a table was made by British chemist John Newlands in 1864. He listed the elements by atomic weight and noticed certain properties recurring every eighth place. He called it the law of octaves (after the musical term), but his idea was incomplete because the recurrence was limited to a small number of elements. Newlands was on the right track, but there was one secret he didn't know about. It would take a longhaired revolutionary from Siberia to unravel the secret and create the first periodic table of the elements.

## Who was Dmitry Mendeleyev?

Dmitry Mendeleyev was born the youngest of 14 children in Tobolsk, Siberia, in 1834. His family had been pioneers in desolate Siberia, starting the first printing press, the first newspaper, and the first glass factory. Russia had been under the strict rule of monarchs called czars, since the sixteenth century and revolutionaries were starting to demand government reforms and more freedom. These political enemies of the czar were often exiled to Siberia as punishment for their activities. One of these exiles married one of Mendeleyev's sisters and taught the eager young Mendeleyev natural science.

In his late teens, Mendeleyev faced a series of setbacks that would threaten his future. His father died and the family's glass factory burned down. Mendeleyev's mother decided to take her son to St. Petersburg to further his education. He quickly had to learn to speak Russian rather than his Siberian dialect to complete his degree. After college his mother died, and he was told he had six months to live due to a lung condition. Luckily, the doctors were wrong, and in 1865 Mendeleyev was made a professor of chemistry at St. Petersburg University. It was here just eight years later that Mendeleyev would devise his periodic table of the elements.

### How did Mendeleyev arrange his new periodic table of the elements?

There were several reasons why Mendeleyev was able to put together a remarkably accurate periodic table. First, he used the new atomic weights calculated by Italian chemist Stanislao Cannizzaro. (Cannizzaro had taken the new figures to the Karlsruhe Convention of chemists in 1860 to defend the still-unknown Avogadro and his molecular laws.) Then, Mendeleyev spent several years researching and experimenting to verify the properties that the elements were supposed to have. He also made the assumption that the elements were a puzzle with many pieces (undiscovered elements) still missing.

Mendeleyev started by grouping the elements based on similar properties, such as how they react with oxygen. This gave him seven groups of atoms. He then found he

*After becoming a teacher, Mendeleyev found he was dissatisfied with the chemistry textbooks available to his students. He wrote his own textbook, **Principles of Chemistry**, in just 60 days. Writing this book for his students was the beginning of his research for the periodic table.*

This photograph of Dmitry Mendeleyev was taken in his later years. Mendeleyev developed the first periodic table of elements when he was quite young.

could easily arrange each of these groups according to atomic weight in vertical columns. This created a pattern where all the atoms could be arranged according to *both* weight and properties. He made the bold claim that "properties of the elements were periodic functions of their atomic weights." Mendeleyev called his table the periodic table of the elements because the chemical properties repeated themselves periodically every seven elements.

# Changes to Mendeleyev's Periodic Table

Considering all the discoveries that have been made since Mendeleyev devised his periodic table, there have been few changes to his table. Fifty new elements have been added as they have been discovered, but the main change had to do with a new measure of the atom, the atomic number.

но въ ней, мнѣ кажется, уже ясно выражается примѣнимость выставляемаго мною начала ко всей совокупности элементовъ, паи которыхъ извѣстенъ съ достовѣрностію. На этотъ разъ я и желалъ преимущественно найдти общую систему элементовъ. Вотъ этотъ опытъ:

|  |  |  | Ti=50 | Zr=90 | ?=180. |
|---|---|---|---|---|---|
|  |  |  | V=51 | Nb=94 | Ta=182. |
|  |  |  | Cr=52 | Mo=96 | W=186. |
|  |  |  | Mn=55 | Rh=104,4 | Pt=197,4 |
|  |  |  | Fe=56 | Ru=104,4 | Ir=198. |
|  |  | Ni=Co=59 | | Pl=106,6 | Os=199. |
| H=1 | | | Cu=63,4 | Ag=108 | Hg=200. |
|  | Be=9,4 | Mg=24 | Zn=65,2 | Cd=112 | |
|  | B=11 | Al=27,4 | ?=68 | Ur=116 | Au=197? |
|  | C=12 | Si=28 | ?=70 | Sn=118 | |
|  | N=14 | P=31 | As=75 | Sb=122 | Bi=210 |
|  | O=16 | S=32 | Se=79,4 | Te=128? | |
|  | F=19 | Cl=35,5 | Br=80 | I=127 | |
| Li=7 | Na=23 | K=39 | Rb=85,4 | Cs=133 | Tl=204 |
|  | | Ca=40 | Sr=87,6 | Ba=137 | Pb=207. |
|  | | ?=45 | Ce=92 | | |
|  | | ?Er=56 | La=94 | | |
|  | | ?Yt=60 | Di=95 | | |
|  | | ?In=75,6 | Th=118? | | |

а потому приходится въ разныхъ рядахъ имѣть различное измѣненіе разностей, чего нѣтъ въ главныхъ числахъ предлагаемой таблицы. Или же придется предполагать при составленіи системы очень много недостающихъ членовъ. То и другое мало выгодно. Мнѣ кажется притомъ, наиболѣе естественнымъ составить кубическую систему (предлагаемая есть плоскостная), но и попытки для ея образованія не повели къ надлежащимъ результатамъ. Слѣдующія двѣ попытки могутъ показать то разнообразіе сопоставленій, какое возможно при допущеніи основнаго начала, высказаннаго въ этой статьѣ.

| Li | Na | K | Cu | Rb | Ag | Cs | — | Tl |
|---|---|---|---|---|---|---|---|---|
| 7 | 23 | 39 | 63,4 | 85,4 | 108 | 133 | | 204 |
| Be | Mg | Ca | Zn | Sr | Cd | Ba | — | Pb |
| B | Al | — | — | Ur | | — | — | Bi? |
| C | Si | Ti | — | Zr | Sn | — | — | — |
| N | P | V | As | Nb | Sb | — | Ta | — |
| O | S | — | Se | — | Te | — | W | — |
| F | Cl | — | Br | — | J | — | — | — |
| 19 | 35,5 | 58 | 80 | 190 | 127 | 160 | 190 | 220. |

Mendeleyev's first periodic table, shown right, was a brilliant way of organizing knowledge that led other scientists to think in new ways and predict the discovery of new elements. The modern table, showing the new elements, appears on the next page.

## How was Mendeleyev's periodic table especially brilliant?

Mendeleyev was convinced he had uncovered the chemical "order" of the universe, but he had two problems. First, there were gaps in the table—places where elements were needed to complete the group. Mendeleyev simply said these were elements that had not yet been discovered. He said they would be discovered soon, and he

In 1913, the British chemist Henry Moseley discovered that a few of Mendeleyev's elements were slightly out of place. He solved the problem by rearranging the elements according to the atomic number. The atomic number is the number of smaller particles, called protons, in an atom of the element. The atomic number measures the electrical charge in the atom, which directly determines the identity of the element. The order of the elements by atomic number is only slightly different from Mendeleyev's order by atomic weight.

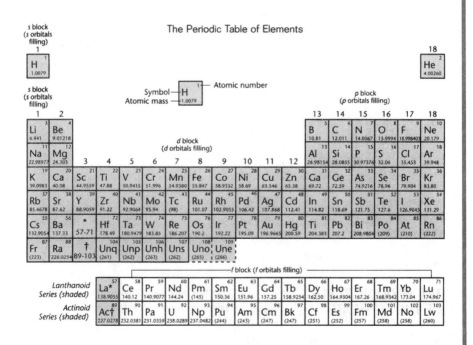

The Periodic Table of Elements

*The German chemist Julius Lothar Meyer worked out a very similar periodic table at about the same time as Mendeleyev. He published his findings in 1870, one year after Mendeleyev.*

predicted the atomic weights and the properties those elements would have. Six years later, the French chemist Paul-Émile Lecoq de Boisbaudran discovered the first of these missing elements. He called the element gallium (from the Latin *gallia* meaning "France") and it had almost all the properties Mendeleyev had predicted. The other missing elements would soon be discovered also.

The other problem made Mendeleyev doubt his entire arrangement. Two elements, tellurium and gold, seemed to be in the wrong place. Based on their atomic weights, they were in groups with different properties. Mendeleyev made another bold decision: their atomic weights must be wrong. He placed them in the group he thought they belonged in and estimated what their correct atomic weights should be. Further experiments proved him to be right again: their atomic weights had been miscalculated.

### Who was Madame Curie?

She had one of the most difficult lives of any of the amazing scientists in this book. Her mother died when she was just 10 years old. She was forced to leave her homeland because women were not allowed to attend college. She lived in poverty during her college years, often barely surviving on bread and tea. Her research was conducted in a rundown shack with little heat and a leaky roof. For several years, the work consisted of boiling and stirring large vats of a dirtlike ore. The fumes gave her a case of pneumonia that laid her up for months and nearly killed her. Her husband died after just 11 years of marriage when he was run over by a horse-drawn carriage. Radiation from the chemicals she studied was slowly poisoning her, but she did not know it. It eventually killed her.

*Marie Curie won two Nobel Prizes for her work, one for physics and one for chemistry. She was the first woman to win a Nobel Prize and the first person to win two.*

Madame Curie was born Maria Sklodowska in Warsaw, Poland, in 1867. Russia ruled Poland at the time and was trying to eliminate Polish culture. Even speaking the Polish language was against the law, but most parents taught their children their native language in secret. Curie's parents were both teachers and placed a high value on education, but when Curie graduated high school at 15, she had few opportunities.

Curie spent the next eight years as a governess while her sister completed her medical studies in Paris. In 1891, she went to Paris and became a science student at the Sorbonne. Within just four years, she earned graduate degrees in both physics and mathematics. She also married the well-known French physicist Pierre Curie and changed her name to Marie. The research she conducted to earn her doctorate made Marie Curie famous. Her scientific career basically consisted of the discovery of one element, but it was enough to immortalize her.

### How did the unfinished experiment of a French scientist inspire Marie Curie?

In 1895, the German physicist Wilhelm Roentgen discovered X rays, a radiation that could penetrate most solid materials and expose photographic plates. Also, any gas, such as air, became electrified when struck by these rays. (The discovery eventually led to the use of X rays to take pictures of the inside of the human body to diagnose disease.) The French scientist Henri Becquerel decided to investigate whether these X rays had anything to do with **fluorescence,** the glowing of materials when exposed to ultraviolet light like sunlight.

*The Curies could have become multimillionaires from their discovery of radium, but they refused. They said the element and its benefits belonged to the people.*

One fluorescent element he experimented with was uranium. He wrapped some photographic film in black paper so sunlight could not expose it, placed a crystal of

Marie Curie's discoveries in the field of radioactivity earned her a Nobel Prize in science; her daughter Irène also won one, making them the only mother-daughter winners in Nobel history.

uranium on the paper, and exposed it to sunlight. The radiation from the uranium developed the film. He then found that the uranium did not even need the sunlight; it exposed the film in total darkness. Clearly, the uranium was emitting a radiation all its own even more penetrating than X rays. Becqueral did not pursue his study of this radiation, but he did tell Marie Curie about it.

### How did Curie find the source of this new radiation?

Most scientific funding at the time was going toward the study of X rays. Curie was much more interested in this new radiation and its source. The Curies were poor, so they had to take the only "lab" available to them—a cold, rundown shack near the Sorbonne.

Curie's first step in her research was to find all the sources for this radiation and then choose the strongest for her research. Pierre Curie had invented a device called the electrometer, which measured radiation levels. Marie tested all the elements and hundreds of minerals, especially uranium compounds. She found that compounds of another element, thorium, emitted similar rays, but her most exciting discovery was one property of a uranium

## The Harmful Effects of Radium

It was not until the 1920s that scientists became aware of the dangers of working with radioactivity. Radioactive rays hold an incredible amount of fast-moving energy and easily penetrate human tissue. Once inside the body, the rays damage or destroy cells at a rapid rate. Radioactive substances can affect human bodies in different, unpredictable ways and from far away. Some people are affected more slowly than others.

Curie spent the final 15 years of her life running the new Radium Institute in Paris. The Institute researched medical uses of radiation, but by the 1920s several workers had died of cancer. Curie refused to believe that the radiation caused the cancers and never investigated its health hazards. She died in 1934 of leukemia at the age of 67, a disease almost certainly brought on by her years of exposure to radiation.

ore called pitchblende. This ore emitted a much stronger radiation than uranium alone. Curie decided there must be one or more new elements in the ore that were "radioactive," as she called it.

Luckily, Austria had tons of pitchblende, which was considered unusable once the uranium had been removed. The ore was delivered to Curie's shack, and she started boiling and refining it to separate all its elements. It took years of horrible, backbreaking work (Pierre was now assisting her), but amazing results eventually came. First, she discovered a new radioactive element and named it polonium after Poland. It was 400 times stronger than uranium, but that was just the start.

Another element was hiding in the ore, and by 1898 Curie had found it. She named it radium (from the Latin for "shedding rays"). It took four more years to purify it and determine its atomic weight, but radium proved even more remarkable than she had imagined. It was one million times stronger than uranium. It gave off heat and glowed blue in the dark. It produced radioactive gases. It made impressions on photographic plates and turned its glass containers violet. It was also deadly.

## What were the consequences of Curie's discovery of radium?

Curie discovered that a minute amount of radium would destroy human tissue. This meant it would be tremendously effective in treating many types of cancer by destroying cancerous tumors. Doctors immediately started treating cancer patients with radiotherapy, or Curie therapy as it was sometimes called. There was a problem, however. Many years later, it was discovered that prolonged exposure to radiation was very dangerous. Many radiation researchers died until safeguards were taken to limit their exposure.

The discovery was important to the science world also. First, Curie showed that the measurement of radiation was a new way to find new elements. Perhaps Curie's most vital discovery of all was that radiation was not the result of a chemical reaction but a property of an element. In fact, she theorized correctly that the source of the radiation was from inside the atom. This realization would

*Radium is less than one millionth a part of pitchblende. Even after several years of shoveling, boiling, and filtering tons of ore, Curie still only found 0.1 gram of pure radium.*

*Curie's daughter Irène won a Nobel Prize in 1935 for discovering the first artificial radioactive element. Like her mother, she developed leukemia from radiation exposure, and died in 1956 at the age of 58.*

mark a change of scientific focus from chemistry to physics and would have a huge influence on the great atomic scientists of the twentieth century like British physicist Ernest Rutherford (see page 101 for more on Rutherford) and American physicist Albert Einstein (see page 105 for more on Einstein). It would also lead to a greater understanding of the structure of the atom and the incredible power that lay within it.

### How did the cell theory develop?

By the 1850s, people still didn't know exactly what caused disease. There were many theories, but none were based on scientific principles. In 1858, the German physician Rudolf Virchow offered the first clue with his cell theory. He said the cell (which Dutch inventor Antoni van Leeuwenhoek had seen 200 years earlier) was the basic unit of human life and that disease occurs when the function of cells is disrupted. From this, he developed the science of **pathology,** the study of diseased body tissue.

Virchow applied his cell theory to both diseased and healthy tissue and asserted that diseased cells are produced by healthy cells. For example, the first malignant cell in cancer is born from a healthy cell. It's called a mutation, and it produces more cancerous cells. Virchow proposed that a study of cells would explain what causes disease in the body. Twenty-five years later, another German physician would use Virchow's ideas to discover the chemistry behind disease and create a "magic bullet" to fight the process.

### Who was Paul Ehrlich?

Paul Ehrlich was born in Strehlin, Germany, in 1854. He received his medical degree from the University of Leipzig in 1878, but he was much more interested in research than opening up a practice. At the time, French chemist Louis Pasteur and German bacteriologist Robert Koch were each discovering the role bacteria played in disease, but Ehrlich was the first to think of chemistry in relation to medicine.

Ehrlich was fascinated by dyes and how they could be used to stain certain tissues and cells in the body. Ehrlich's

*The biggest breakthrough in antibiotics came in 1928 when British bacteriologist Alexander Fleming discovered penicillin. Penicillin is a nonpoisonous chemical produced by mold that kills many different bacteria.*

A photograph of Paul Ehrlich shows him working with test tubes in the early 1900s. His research made antibiotics and chemotherapy possible and practical.

idea was that if a chemical like a dye could combine only with certain cells, then a chemical like a drug could combine only with disease-causing cells, like bacteria. The drug could then kill the bacteria without harming the tissue around it, like a "magic bullet." It was the beginning of chemotherapy, the treatment of disease using drugs.

### How did antibodies help Ehrlich discover his magic bullets?

In 1890, another German researcher Emil von Behring, discovered that the blood of animals infected with different diseases contained chemicals that attacked the disease cells. He called these chemicals **antibodies** and found that

*In his cellular research, Ehrlich discovered six different blood cell types. Because of this, he is considered the founder of modern hematology, the study of blood.*

they often provided immunity, or lifetime protection, against a disease after the first attack. Ehrlich realized that this was how his dyes worked—the dyes only colored certain cells, and the antibodies attacked only certain kinds of cells without harming other tissue. He started working with Behring to find how antibodies work and if they could somehow be produced outside the body.

Ehrlich discovered that foreign bodies, like bacteria or poisons, contain protein molecules he called **antigens.** When the human body senses that an antigen is present, it makes antibodies to make the substance harmless. Ehrlich called the battle between the two substances an immune response and wondered if he could make an organism produce antibodies by deliberately infecting animals with certain germs.

Behring and Ehrlich infected some horses with the bacteria that cause diphtheria, a very contagious, often fatal, respiratory disease that usually attacks children. Blood was then taken from the horses, and the antibodies were concentrated into an antitoxin. An antitoxin is a medicine that contains antibodies to neutralize the toxic, or poisonous, effect of bacteria. This antitoxin medicine could be injected into humans to create immunity to the disease without contracting the disease first.

Ehrlich later explained exactly how antibodies work in his side chain theory. He said that antibodies grew many "arms," which he called receptors, to grab the foreign bodies. The structures of the antigen in the foreign body and the antibody receptors fit together like a lock and key. This is how the antibodies destroy bacteria without harming surrounding tissue. Sometimes the receptors break off from the antibodies and attack foreign bodies by themselves. Ehrlich had found his "magic bullets."

*Ehrlich once caught tuberculosis while studying the bacterium that causes the disease. He had to spend two years in the warm, dry air of Egypt to recover.*

### What about diseases that antibodies couldn't handle?

The human body's immune response, using its own antibodies, was still not enough for many diseases. Common diseases like malaria, sleeping sickness, and syphilis are caused by bacteria and other infectious germs that the body's "magic bullets" cannot destroy. Ehrlich set

## The Future of Antibiotics

A drug that kills bacteria is referred to as an antibiotic. Many antibiotics have been developed since Ehrlich founded chemotherapy and Alexander Fleming discovered the first antibiotic, penicillin, in 1928. There is a growing problem, however, with the use of antibiotics. They have been overused.

Just as humans develop immunity to diseases, bacteria develop immunity to antibiotics. Over the years, the bacteria cells have mutated, or changed into new forms that are resistant to antibiotics. Some diseases, like tuberculosis and malaria, were once very easy to cure and had nearly disappeared. Their infectious germs have now mutated into resistant forms, and cures are more difficult. This is why scientists need to keep developing new drugs to fight disease.

out to create chemical "magic bullets" that would cure these kinds of diseases. He called it chemotherapy, meaning medical treatment with chemicals, or drugs. (Chemotherapy today means a specific kind of treatment for cancer, while Ehrlich's "magic bullets" are simply called antibiotics. They are just one kind of prescription drug now available to fight disease.)

In the early 1900s, syphilis was a major public health concern. The horrible disease was contagious and attacked internal organs and the central nervous system. It caused blindness, paralysis, insanity, and often death. The bacterium that caused syphilis had just been discovered, so Ehrlich decided to look for a "magic bullet" for syphilis first.

Ehrlich started experimenting with an arsenic chemical. Arsenic is poisonous so it would destroy bacteria and other infectious germs, but it would have to be mixed with other chemicals to make it safe for other tissue. Ehrlich tried combination after combination. On his 606th chemical, he was successful. The drug cured animals infected with syphilis bacteria without harming the animals. It was the first chemical drug in the history of medicine.

*Syphilis first appeared in Spain in 1493 among sailors who returned from the voyage of Christopher Columbus to the New World. Over the centuries, it spread to millions of people before Ehrlich discovered the cure.*

Ehrlich named the drug Salvarsan (safe arsenic) and took it to an insane asylum nearby to test it on humans. Many syphilis victims wound up in the insane asylum due to the disease's horrible effects. Some were already near death when Ehrlich arrived, but Salvarsan cured every syphilis patient. "Magic bullets" could be made outside of the body. Many diseases that used to cause suffering and death could now be cured with drugs.

Who was Sir Isaac Newton? ◆ How did an apple falling
from a treen enhance our understanding of the uni
verse? ◆ What are Newton's three fundamental law
of motion? ◆ How did Newton's study of optics lead to
a better teles ◆ Wh d co e ectromagnet
sm? ◆ Who was Michael Faraday? ◆ How did Farada
convert ma ism to electricity? ◆ W Which theor
of Faraday's was so advanced that it influenced twen
tieth-century physicists? ◆ What great but unknown
scientist influenced Faraday's ideas on magnetism? ◆
Who was James Clerk Maxwell? ◆ How did Maxwel
turn Faraday's field theory into a map of the universe

# AMAZING
# PHYSICISTS

### Who was Sir Isaac Newton?

In 1665, the bubonic plague swept over London,
England, killing tens of thousands of people. To try to
stop the spread of the disease, students were sent home
from universities and were not able to return for 18
months. The time was a tragedy for England, but an amazing leap forward for the science world. In those 18
months, the laws of gravitation, motion, and optics were
discovered and a new mathematical system called calculus was invented. What's even more remarkable is that
this was all accomplished by one man, a 23-year-old student who had been sent home because of the plague.

Isaac Newton was born on a farm outside London in
1642, the year the Italian scientist Galileo (see page 124
for more on Galileo) died. As a child, all he wanted to do
was build models, and he became ingenious at it. By the
time he was a teenager, he was building intricate wind-
mills, water clocks, sundials, and flying lanterns. At 18, he
was sent to Cambridge, where he adopted his lifelong
approach to science: asking the questions that no one had
yet answered.

Newton answered many of those questions in the
months at his family's farm, but most of the science world
would not know about it for 20 years. Newton had no
interest in publishing his findings. Once he had made a

Sir Issac Newton experiments with a prism and a ray of light. His work with light advanced the knowledge of optics and physics.

discovery and had used it in his own research, he was done with it. Once the world did find out, it would never be the same.

*At almost the same time Newton was developing his system of calculus, the mathematician Gottfried Wilhelm Leibniz was developing a similar system in Germany.*

## How did an apple falling from a tree enhance our understanding of the universe?

Newton's first discovery concerned gravity. Scientists knew of gravity, and Johannes Kepler (see page 120 for more on Kepler) had theorized that it had something to do with the movement of the planets, but this was not enough for Newton. When he saw an apple fall from a tree at his family's farm, he wanted to know the laws at work and to find the mathematical formulas to show how the laws worked.

Newton realized immediately he needed a new system of mathematics for his calculations. He invented **calculus,** a system that uses symbols and numbers to measure infinitesimal and changing quantities. The laws of gravity were no longer a mystery. Newton discovered that the entire universe is held together by gravity. Every object attracts every other object, and the force can be calculated using the mass of the objects and the distance between them—the greater the mass, the greater the attraction, and the greater the distance, the weaker the attraction.

Once astronomers had Newton's formulas for gravitational pull, they could account for all the known movements of the solar system. The English astronomer Edmond Halley was the scientist who first found out about Newton's discoveries and urged him to publish his findings. Halley used Newton's formulas to predict that a comet that had appeared in 1682 would reappear in 1758. The comet returned in 1758 and became known as Halley's comet.

### What are Newton's three fundamental laws of motion?

Newton finally published his scientific breakthroughs in 1687 in a three-volume set called *Principia Mathematica*. It took him three years to write down his vast store of knowledge, but the book was immediately recognized at the time as the most important scientific work ever written. It was also the beginning of the science of **mechanics,** the study of how forces act on matter.

The *Principia* includes Newton's three laws of motion, the foundation of mechanics. The first law introduces the

*Putting together all the information contained in the* **Principia** *exhausted Newton so much that he suffered a nervous breakdown and needed two years to recuperate.*

## A Mind Like No Other

In 1696, the Swiss mathematician Johann Bernoulli challenged the scientists of the world to solve a problem he proposed. It was a very difficult problem, so he allowed six months for the solution. At the end of the six months, there were no solutions. The German mathematician, Gottfried Wilhelm Leibniz, who is given credit along with Newton for inventing calculus, thought he was close and requested two more months. He was granted the extension but was still unable to solve the problem.

The problem was published in a science journal and brought to the attention of Newton. He sat down and solved the problem in one night. He submitted the answer anonymously, but it wasn't hard for Bernoulli to realize who had solved it. He said, "I recognize the claw of the lion."

concept of **inertia:** an object at rest will remain at rest and an object in motion will remain in motion at a constant speed unless influenced by an outside force. For example, friction will slow down objects in motion on Earth, and Earth would spin out of orbit without the Sun's gravity pulling it back.

The second law states that an object will move in the direction of an outside force applied to it and its motion is proportional to the amount of force applied. For example, if you throw a ball easily, it may travel 20 feet forward; if you throw it hard, it may travel 100 feet forward. Even as late as 1687, no one had stated this law of motion before.

The third law states that for every action, there is an opposite and equal reaction. For example, a rocket will lift off the ground after the ignition of its engine propels hot gases downward.

*Although Newton built the most sophisticated telescope of his time, he never made any systematic observations of the skies.*

### How did Newton's study of optics lead to a better telescope?

Newton had tried for years to build a better telescope. Like most astronomers of the day, he was troubled by the blurry images and the halos of color that lenses produced. He turned to a study of light to try to resolve the problem.

In Newton's time, prisms were sold as toys because people liked to see the colors they produced when sunlight passed through them. It was believed that white was the pure light and that the colors were some kind of variation on the white light. Newton used these toys to discover the basic principles of light.

*Newton was not always right. He incorrectly believed in alchemy, the science of changing base metals into gold.*

Newton used a lens to focus the band of colors, or the spectrum as he called it, that the prism produced. He found that each color was **refracted,** or bent, at a particular angle no matter how the prism was positioned. Newton added a second prism to the experiment and discovered that none of the colors of the spectrum could be altered in any way. He concluded that they were the fundamental colors of light and that white light was a combination of all the other colors.

This also explained why the telescopes of Newton's time produced blurred images surrounded with color. The lenses inside the telescopes were not refracting light to one sharp focus. Newton had heard that a mirror with a specially shaped surface **reflected,** or bounced back, light to a single focus without the colors of a lens. He built a telescope replacing one of the lenses with a mirror, and the images were much clearer and had no color halos. These Newtonian telescopes are still built today using the same method.

## Who discovered electromagnetism?

In 1820, the Danish scientist Hans Christian Ørsted was conducting an experiment with an electrical circuit. He noticed that when he turned the circuit on and off, a nearby compass needle jumped. He concluded that electricity produces magnetism, and the science of electromagnetism was born.

The finding was interesting, but one English scientist realized it would be much more helpful to know if magnetism could be made to produce electricity. The Industrial Revolution was in full swing and England needed new sources of power to run its new machines. In the decade after Ørsted's discovery, other scientists tried without success to produce electricity from magnetism. In 1831, a self-taught research assistant at England's Royal Institution found the solution after just 10 days of experimentation.

## Who was Michael Faraday?

Michael Faraday was born in 1791 in Newington, near London, England. His father was a blacksmith and the family was very poor. There were times when the young Faraday had only bread to eat. Faraday's family belonged to a small Christian sect called the Sandemanians. Its founder, Robert Sandeman, believed that the greatest achievement a person could have in life was to "add to mankind's knowledge of God's universe." Despite this, Faraday's formal education consisted only of learning the three Rs—reading, writing, and arithmetic—at Sunday school.

At 13, even that education ended and Faraday became an apprentice to a bookbinder. It was the turning point in

*Faraday coined all the following electrical terms: electrode, anode, cathode, electrolyte, and ion.*

An 1858 photograph of Michael Faraday, who constructed the first electric generator by working with magnets and wire.

his life. In his new job, he was able to read many books, especially the science books he loved so much. In 1810, Faraday attended a series of lectures by England's most famous scientist, Sir Humphry Davy. Faraday was so impressed with Davy that he wrote the great scientist asking for a job and included the notes he had taken on Davy's lectures. Davy hired him and many years later would admit, "The greatest of all my discoveries is Faraday."

### How did Faraday convert magnetism to electricity?

The experiment Faraday devised to bring about the conversion of magnetism to electricity, or **induction,** sounds very simple. In time, it led to the huge generators used today to make electric power. First, Faraday made a conductor for the electricity by winding 220 feet of copper wire around a cardboard cylinder. The ends of the wire were connected to a **galvanometer,** an instrument that detects electricity. He then simply pushed a bar magnet into the cylinder and saw the needle on the galvanometer jump. When he removed the magnet, the needle jumped again in the opposite direction.

This proved that magnetism produces electricity, but Faraday was disappointed. He was looking for a constant flow, not just a jolt. He noticed that if he kept pushing the magnet in and out of the cylinder, the needle kept jumping. It was the motion between the conductor and the magnet that created a constant flow. The solution to that problem would be almost as simple.

Faraday mounted a large copper disk about 1 foot in diameter and ¼ inch thick on a brass axle. He placed it between the poles of the largest magnet he could find. Then he attached two pieces of copper to the apparatus so that one was in contact with the copper disk and one was in contact with the brass axle, like brushes. The copper brushes were attached to an electric meter. He attached a handle to the brass axle and made the axle spin. It worked. This was the first electric generator.

*Faraday's work with Davy led to Faraday's laws of electrolysis. Electrolysis is using electricity to decompose compounds into their elements. Davy had discovered many elements in this way, including potassium, sodium, and calcium.*

## Which theory of Faraday's was so advanced that it influenced twentieth-century physicists?

One simple experiment students often conduct is to place two magnets on a table with opposite poles facing each other but not touching. A piece of paper is placed on top of the magnets and iron filings are dropped on top of the paper above the magnets. Friction keeps the iron filings from moving much, but if the paper is tapped lightly, the filings twist their way toward the magnets in lines. The lines directly between the magnets are straight, and the lines farther outside the magnets are curved.

Scientists had noticed this phenomenon for centuries, but Faraday saw tremendous meaning in it. He called the lines "magnetic lines of force" and said they moved outward great distances from the poles. He said this is why a compass would work such a great distance from Earth's polar regions. Faraday measured the strengths of these magnetic fields and observed the different directions of the lines. He did not have the mathematical training to study them further, however.

Faraday thought other forces, like gravity, electricity, and even light, all acted with these lines of force, or fields. He took the theory one step further and said that matter itself extended beyond its visible edges and filled all space. We know there are gravitational and electrical fields but Faraday's theory was so advanced that some of it is still being tested today. The twentieth-century physicist Albert Einstein (see page 105 for more on Einstein) used field theory in much of his work and another field has now been discovered. The forces around the nucleus of the atom are known as nuclear fields.

*Faraday studied electric fish, like electric eels, very closely and measured the strength of their electrical shock. He found that, like a battery, electric fish have a positive end in their head and a negative end in their tail.*

## What great but unknown scientist influenced Faraday's ideas on magnetism?

The beginnings of Faraday's ideas about magnetism started over 200 years before in a book titled *Of Magnets* by English scientist William Gilbert. It was published in 1600 and was probably the first great scientific work written in England.

Gilbert was a remarkable scientist who was centuries ahead of his time in many fields. He lived during the age of exploration, so he undertook the study of magnetism to try to come up with a better compass and other navigational tools. He was the first to study the lines of force around magnets, which became Faraday's fields. He theorized that Earth was a large magnet and exerted a magnetic influence (gravity) throughout the solar system. He

## Merry Christmas, Mrs. Faraday!

On Christmas morning in 1821, Michael Faraday had an unusual present for his wife. He led her to his laboratory, where he presented her with one of his experiments, but she had no idea what it was. There was a small container of mercury with a magnet attached to it. A copper rod was placed above the magnet, with one end stuck in a cork that floated on the mercury. Finally, a battery was connected to the upper end of the copper rod and to the mercury.

When the battery was connected and the circuit was complete, the copper rod started revolving above the magnet. It was the first electric motor, but inventors did not start making electric toys yet. Electricity was too expensive—Faraday hadn't invented an easy way of producing it yet. That would come 10 years later, with his research or induction.

was the first scientist to use the term "electric" to describe one substance's power to attract other objects. He made the first electroscope, an instrument that detects the presence of an electric charge.

Gilbert was also the first scientist in England to support the Copernican system of the universe, and he rejected the idea that the stars were all the same distance from Earth. He was also personal physician to Queen Elizabeth I and King James I.

## Who was James Clerk Maxwell?

The substance was different from all other matter. It couldn't be seen or felt or even measured, but it was present everywhere. It existed throughout space and even in vacuums. It was stationary and all bodies in space traveled through it. Its basic property was that it was **luminiferous** —it could carry light. It was called ether, and scientists in the eighteenth and nineteenth centuries used it to explain how light traveled.

The scientists knew that light travels in waves through vacuums and the void of space. What they thought they needed was a medium, or substance, for it to travel through just as sound waves need air to travel. The idea of ether filled their need. One of the most brilliant scientists who ever lived would disprove the ether theory even though he still believed in it.

James Clerk Maxwell was born in Edinburgh, Scotland, in 1831. Maxwell's mother died when he was very young, so his eccentric father took over his upbringing, even schooling him until he was 10. Maxwell showed an early interest in geometry and mechanical models and submitted his first scientific paper to the Royal Society of Edinburgh when he was only 14.

Maxwell entered Edinburgh University at 16, and his odd habits earned him the nickname "Dafty." He eventually received his degree in mathematics from Cambridge University in 1854 and started a career in research that would include important findings in optics, astronomy, chemistry, and mathematics. His most important work, however, would come in electromagnetism. When Maxwell applied his mathematics to Michael Faraday's field theory, the world of physics was transformed.

*When Albert Einstein (see page 105 for more on Einstein) drew his new picture of the universe in the twentieth century, he started with Maxwell's model of electromagnetic fields.*

### How did Maxwell turn Faraday's field theory into a map of the universe?

Faraday studied the lines that iron filings formed by magnets and saw lines of force spreading across the universe. He thought other forces, like gravity, electricity, and even light, all acted with these lines of force. He was right, but he could not work out the mathematical proof, or description, of his theory. Maxwell put together the model and the mathematical equations that proved Faraday's theory.

First, Maxwell showed that magnetic fields and electric fields always exist together, so the field is really an electromagnetic field. Maxwell's model for this electromagnetic field that spreads out in all directions in the universe is complicated. It can best be described as a series of rotating cylinders separated by small spheres. When one cylinder turns, the motion is transmitted through the spheres so that all the cylinders turn like a whirlpool. The field is a loop around the universe with no starting or ending point.

Maxwell's equations are even more complicated, but they basically have to do with measurable electrical and magnetic quantities of mass, distance, and time. He found that electric waves and magnetic waves travel because of the effects they have on each other. His equations also revealed that electromagnetic waves travel at the speed of light. Maxwell concluded that light itself was electromagnetic radiation and he suggested that there were probably many other forms of electromagnetic radiation, that we cannot see. The German physicist Heinrich Hertz discovered the first of these, radio waves, in 1888.

### What was Maxwell's kinetic theory of gases?

In 1798, the British scientist Benjamin Thompson, Count Rumford, proved that heat was a form of motion, not the weightless fluid of previous theories. By Maxwell's time, it was known that it was the atoms or molecules of the hot substance that were moving, but what was the nature of the movement? Did the atoms and molecules of cool substances also move? Did they all move at the same speed, or was the motion random? If molecules move

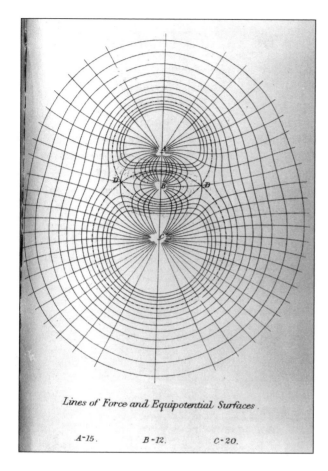

Lines of Force and Equipotential Surfaces.

A-15.      B-12.      C-20.

James Clerk Maxwell drew this diagram showing the lines of force of three different size objects. Maxwell's theories were most often expressed in mathematical formulas that eventually related the three main fields of physics—electricity, magnetism and light—to one another.

randomly, how can there be any scientific laws concerning them? Maxwell had an answer and, as usual he turned to mathematics to explain it.

Maxwell studied gases and assumed that their molecules were moving randomly. Maxwell first worked out an equation that showed the range of velocities (speed and direction of speed) gas molecules would have at any given temperature. He then showed that gases store heat in the motion of their molecules. As a gas is heated, its molecules move faster and push each other farther apart. This means the gas expands. If the temperature of the gas decreases, the gas contracts.

Maxwell was even able to calculate the size of gas molecules and apply his mathematical theory of gas molecules to other properties of gases. His kinetic theory

## The Composition of Saturn's Rings

One of the first questions Maxwell tackled concerned the composition of Saturn's rings. Are they solid or composed of countless separate particles? Maxwell first theorized that the rings could not be either uniformly solid or liquid because they would be unstable and would break up. He used mathematics to indicate that the only possible way a ring would not collide with the surface of Saturn would be to have about 82 percent of its mass packed onto one side. However, he said such a precise packing was highly unlikely since the rings had formed at random.

Maxwell concluded that the only possibility was that the rings were composed of a large number of small satellites, each orbiting Saturn independently. The theory was finally confirmed after the Pioneer and Voyager spacecrafts took photos of the rings in the 1970s and 1980s.

*Maxwell died when he was only 47. He died at the same age and of the same disease, abdominal cancer, as his mother.*

explained the transfer of heat in solids and liquids as well as gases. When a hot substance is placed in contact with a cold substance, its fast-moving molecules collide with the slow-moving cold molecules. The fast molecules slow down and cool down while the slow molecules speed up and heat up. Heat "flows" from the hot substance to the cold one.

What was most remarkable about Maxwell's kinetic theory is that it took random movements but predicted measurable effects. He showed that mathematics could bring order to apparent chaos and explain definite laws of nature.

### Who made the first color photograph in history?

It was Maxwell, and he was only 18 when he made it. While he was still at Edinburgh University, Maxwell decided to study how human eyes detect color. He was very interested in a theory that said that the eye has three types of fibers that are sensitive to the different light waves for red, green, and blue. When light waves strike these fibers, they create electrical signals that travel to the brain. The color sensations that arise in the brain correspond to these electrical signals. British physicist Thomas Young first proposed the theory in 1801.

Maxwell devised a color top with sections painted red, green, and blue to test the theory. He showed that by spinning these primary colors, all other colors could be produced. It was a simple confirmation of Young's theory. Maxwell also proposed that color blindness was simply a defect in one or more of the fibers.

Maxwell's interest in optics continued throughout his life. Several years after his study of color vision, he took the first color photograph in history. He used red, green, and blue filters to expose three frames of film and then combined the images. He then projected the film through the colored filters and produced a color photograph.

## Who was Nikola Tesla?

He was one of the greatest scientific minds in history and one of the most imaginative inventors. Many of his ideas were so far ahead of their time that they remained misunderstood and unstudied. He invented the radio, but the Italian inventor Guglielmo Marconi received credit for it. He discovered X rays, but German physicist Wilhelm Roentgen is remembered as the discoverer. He devised a much better electrical system than did American inventor Thomas Edison, but Edison is much more famous. This American physicist is the greatest scientist few people have ever heard of.

Croatian-born Nikola Tesla was legendary for his eccentricities—and for his profound understanding of electricity.

*When Tesla was a child, he saw a picture of Niagara Falls and told his family that he would go there one day and capture its energy. In 1893, George Westinghouse won the contract to build a power plant at the falls, and he put Tesla in charge.*

Nikola Tesla was born in Smiljan, Croatia, in 1856, and it was clear from the start that he had a brilliant mind. In high school, he was able to perform integral calculus in his head. His teachers thought he was cheating, but he apparently had a photographic memory. He would eventually learn to speak six languages fluently.

Tesla's father was a priest and wanted his son to follow in his footsteps, but Tesla had a passion for physics, mathematics, and engineering. He attended the Polytechnic Institute at Graz, Austria, and immediately became fascinated by electricity. Scientists such as Maxwell had studied electricity and discovered electromagnetic fields throughout the universe. Inventors like Edison studied the practical side of electricity and invented lightbulbs.

Tesla liked both sides and understood electricity better than any man in the world. He had a tremendous new idea for Edison on how to conduct electricity more efficiently and more cheaply. He came to America with his new idea and started to work for Edison. It would be his crowning achievement. It would also be the beginning of his downfall.

### What was Tesla's breakthrough in electricity?

Edison's invention of the lightbulb led to the creation of the Edison Power Company. He had a power plant in New York City, but it was huge and could only transmit power over one square mile through thick, dangerous cables. The problem was that Edison was using DC (direct current) power, a very inefficient source of power. Here's why: electric current loses the least amount of energy when it can travel at high voltages, but high voltages are not safe to use in homes.

Tesla found a solution in **AC (alternating current)** power. An alternating current flows alternately in either direction ,and its voltage can be easily controlled. Tesla showed that AC power could be transmitted efficiently at high voltages and over great distances. When it reached the points where it was to be transferred to homes, devices called transformers could decrease the voltage to safe levels. This is not possible with DC voltage. Tesla also invented all the different components of the entire AC system—generator (for the power plant), transformer, transmission lines, motor (for the home appliances), and lights.

Edison didn't know what Tesla was talking about. He hired Tesla anyway, but the two fought from the start. Tesla even said Edison cheated him out of $50,000 in wages. Tesla took his AC system to Edison's competitor, George Westinghouse, and the "War of the Currents" was on. Edison launched a public campaign against Tesla, calling his AC system dangerous. (The war of words would affect Tesla's reputation the rest of his life—Edison was a highly respected figure in America and the public accepted his beliefs.)

Tesla and Westinghouse would have the last laugh, however. They won the bid to light the 1893 World's Fair in Chicago over Edison and the newly formed General Electric Company. Twelve generators powered 100,000 lights, and the Great Hall of Electricity displayed the AC system for 27 million visitors. Tesla and AC had won the "War of the Currents."

## *Star Wars:* Tesla's Invention to End Warfare

Tesla hated warfare, and one of his dreams was to find a scientific way to end it. He thought it could be reduced to "a mere spectacle of machines." In 1934, he announced that he had found a way to do this. His invention was a weapon that could send through the air "concentrated beams of charged particles so powerful they could bring down a fleet of 10,000 enemy airplanes at a distance of 250 miles."

Tesla tried to get countries around the world interested in his "peace beam" without success.

However, the idea was based on sound scientific ideas. Even today, the United States is working on a system called the Strategic Defense Initiative (SDI). It's an idea very similar to Tesla's, in which any missiles launched toward the United States would be destroyed in the air by charged-particle beams from orbiting satellites.

Tesla did not reveal all the details of his "peace beam." They might have been in his scientific papers, which disappeared right after his death.

### How did Tesla beat Marconi to the discovery of the radio?

Maxwell's findings about electromagnetism in the 1870s and Hertz's discovery of radio waves in the 1880s made Tesla think that the possibilities of electricity were endless. His next research was on high-frequency electricity, but he had a problem. Even his advanced AC generators could only generate a current of about 20,000 cycles per second. (The normal house runs on a 60-cycle-per-second current.) Tesla invented a remarkable device called the Tesla coil, a transformer that changes the frequency of alternating current. He now had access to extremely high frequency electricity—as high as hundreds of thousands of cycles per second.

Tesla's first discoveries with high-frequency electricity were neon lights, fluorescent lights, and X-ray photos (five years before Roentgen). Then he realized he could transmit and receive radio waves if they were tuned to the same frequency. In early 1895, Tesla was ready to demonstrate that he could transmit a radio signal 50 miles between New York City and West Point. Just before the demonstration, his lab burned down, destroying his work. Not long afterward, Marconi (using a Tesla coil) was transmitting across the English Channel and, a few years later, across the Atlantic Ocean.

Tesla waged a legal battle against Marconi for many years over the patent for radio. He had the original patent, but Marconi had powerful businessmen behind him and won the patent in 1904. The Supreme Court eventually reversed the decision in 1943, but Tesla had died a few months before.

Tesla had been disappointed by the failure of his radio demonstration, but he had a bigger idea he wanted to work on. His plan was to build a world system of wireless communications called the Wireless Broadcasting System. The system would send phone messages across the oceans and it would broadcast news, music, weather, and even pictures anywhere in the world. Tesla received $150,000 from financier J. P. Morgan to build a transmission tower and power plant for his system. but the investment was not nearly enough. The project was scrapped and Tesla's reputation never recovered.

## What were some of Tesla's other amazing ideas?

Part of the reason Tesla has remained unappreciated as a scientist is that his ideas were so brilliant that they were far ahead of their time. Here are some examples:

- Tesla discovered the basic science behind radar, the electron microscope, and the microwave oven. Edison called his idea for radar "ridiculous," so it was another 25 years before radar was officially invented.

- He demonstrated the first remote-controlled machine in 1898, starting the science of robotics.

- He was the first man to receive radio signals from outer space. The press called him a "wacko" for this claim. Today's radio telescopes verify that he had received signals from distant stars.

- He created the first, and still the largest, man-made bolt of lightning ever. It was 130 feet long.

- He designed a turbine engine that used disks instead of blades. When built with modern materials, it is still one of the most efficient motors ever designed.

- He said one of his experiments revealed particles with charges smaller than an electron. They're now called quarks, and they were discovered in 1977.

- He predicted today's missiles by contending that one day there would be wingless planes carrying explosives that would be remotely controlled to land in enemy territory.

*Tesla spent his final years as a penniless recluse in a New York hotel. He spent much of his time rescuing injured pigeons from a nearby park.*

*After Tesla's death, many of his scientific papers disappeared. Many researchers have tried unsuccessfully to track them down.*

## Who was Ernest Rutherford?

Science in the twentieth century was dominated by two pursuits: astronomers looked farther and farther into space to the very edge of the universe, and physicists looked deeper and deeper into matter at the smallest particles in the universe. Marie Curie gave the first hints of subatomic particles when she theorized that the atom was the source of radiation.

In 1897, the British physicist Sir Joseph John Thomson announced that he had found particles smaller than the atom. He called them "corpuscles," and he believed that they were scattered throughout the atom like seeds in a watermelon. He was right about the particles, later renamed electrons, but wrong about their properties. It would be one of Thomson's students who would unlock the secrets of the electron and become the first scientist to look inside the atom. In the process, that student would also become the world's first successful alchemist.

Ernest Rutherford was born in Nelson, New Zealand, in 1871. His family were pioneers in the isolated countryside of the new nation, and Rutherford learned the life of a farmer from his father. He was also a bright student, especially in the sciences, and won a scholarship to the University of New Zealand. After college, he was accepted for a research position at Cambridge University, a rare honor for a student from outside of England. The head of physics research at Cambridge was J. J. Thomson and Rutherford was very interested in his "corpuscles."

*Even though Rutherford is considered a physicist, he won the 1908 Nobel Prize for chemistry.*

### What did Rutherford discover about radioactive bullets?

Rutherford agreed with Curie that radioactive rays came from the atom, but what was the nature of these

Ernest Rutherford was about 35 years old when this photograph was taken and had already had success in discovering new aspects of radioactivity. His greatest work, which led to the theory of the atomic nucleus, still lay ahead of him.

subatomic rays? His early research would answer this question. He placed a tray of uranium near the poles of a magnet and placed a photographic plate beyond the magnet. The radiation particles moved quickly between the poles of the magnet, and some went on to strike the photographic plate. When the plate was developed, the points where the particles struck could be examined.

Rutherford detected two different kinds of radiation on the plate. One group of particles was deflected to a much greater degree than the other group and in the opposite direction when passing through the magnetic field. Rutherford also noticed that the particles being deflected the least were much larger and more massive than the others, but the smaller ones moved much more rapidly. He concluded that the particles must have opposite electrical charges.

Using Maxwell's laws of electromagnetism, Rutherford identified the least deflected, more massive particles as positive and the more deflected, faster-moving particles as negative. He called the positive particles alpha radiation and the negative particles beta radiation. (When different radioactive materials were used later, he discovered electrically neutral gamma radiation.) Rutherford had an idea about how these rays could help him look inside the atom: he would use them as microscopic bullets.

*A unit of radioactivity, the rutherford, and element number 104, rutherfordium, were named in Rutherford's honor.*

## How did Rutherford discover what was inside the atom?

In 1908, Rutherford conducted his greatest experiment. First, he directed alpha particles at several different materials and found that they passed through easily. Rutherford beat a piece of gold leaf into a thinness of one fifty-thousandth of an inch. He estimated that the gold leaf was now about 2,000 atoms thick. If atoms filled that space and the atom was indestructible, then the particles would not get through. Again, almost all the particles went through easily, a small number of them were slightly deflected by something, and an even smaller number bounced backward.

Rutherford knew that there was only one conclusion: most of the atom must be empty space that allowed the

## The Length of a Half-Life

Rutherford found that radioactive atoms release radiation in order to take on a more stable form. He called the process radioactive decay. As radioactive elements decay, they change into other elements until they are no longer radioactive, or are stable.

Radioactive decay takes place at different rates in different elements. Rutherford called an element's rate of decay its **half-life**. This is the length of time needed for half the atoms in a sample to decay. For example, the half-life of radium 226 is about 1,600 years. After 1,600 years, one half of the radium in a sample remains. After another 1,600 years, only a fourth remains, and so on. Half-lives of radioactive elements vary from fractions of a second to billions of years.

particles to pass through. He said the positive alpha particles acted just as if they had been repelled by another small, powerful positive charge, a charge concentrated at one point. His model of the atom started at the center with a tiny, positively charged nucleus (from the Latin for "kernel") containing most of the mass of the atom. Since an atom has a neutral charge, he had to also account for a negative charge somewhere in the atom.

He returned to Thomson's electrons, but he knew they were not scattered throughout the atom. He reasoned that the electrons were negatively charged, giving the atom a neutral charge. To account for the vast amount of empty space within the atom, he concluded that the electrons must be a very great distance from the nucleus. He compared it to our solar system with the planets being electrons and the Sun being the nucleus. There were still some details to be worked out, but Rutherford's model was correct. Scientists were now inside the atom.

### Was Rutherford really the first successful alchemist?

In a way, he was. It started in 1901, when Rutherford noticed a strange property of the radioactive element thorium. As thorium gave off radiation, it also produced an invisible gas that was also radioactive. He studied the gas and devised a bold theory. Since radiation particles are coming from inside the atom, the atom changes in structure during the process. If the atom is changing in structure, new elements are formed. Nature is an alchemist.

It was clear to Rutherford that radioactive atoms could spontaneously change into other atoms. This shattered the old idea that atoms cannot change. Several years later, he duplicated the effect in an experiment and became the world's first successful alchemist. The experiment was simple: he aimed alpha particles at nitrogen atoms. The result was the formation of hydrogen atoms and oxygen atoms. It was the first man-made nuclear reaction.

*Beta rays are actually special electrons that form in the nucleus of a radioactive atom and are immediately hurled out.*

The work of British scientist Henry Moseley explains how this experiment worked. Using X rays, Moseley discovered that the nucleus of an atom contains positively charged particles called protons. Heavier elements contain a greater number of protons, and the exact number of these protons is what gives an element its identity. After Moseley's work, Rutherford discovered that an alpha particle was the same as a helium nucleus and contained two protons. When it collided with the nitrogen atom, it donated one of its protons to the nitrogen atom. This changed the nitrogen to oxygen, leaving a leftover single proton, which is hydrogen. It was not the gold alchemists had dreamed of, but years later it would prove much more important than even that.

### Who was Albert Einstein?

One of the most startling discoveries in all scientific history was the amount of energy that is stored in matter. For example, if all the energy that is stored in just one pound of coal could be converted into energy, it would produce the amount of electricity the entire world uses in one day! This is the same principle that led to the development of the atomic bombs of World War II—bombs that destroyed entire cities.

The scientific equation that expresses this principle is the famous $E = mc^2$, and the man who formulated the equation is probably the most famous scientist in history. He changed the way we look at our universe more than any scientist ever had. He also tried very hard to make sure the world would survive his discoveries.

Albert Einstein is famous among the public and scientists alike for his equation $E = mc^2$, his playful side made him popular as an "eccentric" scientific genius.

Albert Einstein was born in Ulm, Germany, in 1879. He was a very slow student and did not like playing games with the other kids. He seemed to prefer to just sit and think. He did not pay much attention to the teachers and hated how they taught the students to learn by rote. This all changed when he studied geometry in high school. He loved how statements needed proof and how problems were solved step-by-step using logic. He decided to devote his life to the study of mathematics.

Einstein attended the famous Federal Polytechnic School in Zurich, Switzerland, and became an outstanding mathematics student. He was also now interested in physics and wanted to devote himself to physics research full-time after graduation. He decided that teaching physics would be the best way to do this.

Einstein graduated in 1905, but he could not obtain a teaching position anywhere. He was forced to accept a menial job as an examiner in a Swiss patent office. Luckily, Einstein had a lot of spare time at his new job— enough to devise his theory of relativity, the most amazing scientific theory ever.

## What was so amazing about Einstein's theory of relativity?

Much of Einstein's theory of **relativity** is baffling even to other scientists. However, the more they studied it, particularly the mathematical equations he offered as proofs, the more they saw how accurate it was. Here are some of its basic points.

Around 1900, the Dutch scientist Hendrik Lorentz worked out a formula showing that as the speed of an electron approaches the speed of light, its mass increases by seven times. This was the beginning of Einstein's theory. He put together some mathematical equations and proved that the mass of any matter, not just electrons, increases with velocity. The change is too small to be noticeable in our visible world, but in the world of atomic and subatomic particles, it's very important. It's important because of Einstein's next finding.

For centuries, two of the fundamental laws of physics were the conservation of matter and the conservation of energy. They state that matter and energy can change in form but cannot be created or destroyed. Discoveries about the behavior of some radioactive elements, like Curie's work with radium, seemed to indicate that the researchers were creating energy. Einstein had an explanation. He said mass is a measure of a substance's "frozen" energy content. When one changes, so does the other. Mass can change into energy and energy can change into mass. He proved it with mathematical equations summed up by $E = mc^2$, where $E$ is energy, $m$ is mass, and $c^2$ is the speed of light times itself. Since the speed of light is around 186,000 miles per second, the equation shows just how much energy is stored in matter.

Another part of the theory dealt with motion and was bold enough to contradict the great Newton. Newton had said in one of his laws of motion that all bodies are either at rest or in uniform motion until an external force acts upon them. Einstein said that it is impossible to determine motion absolutely. Everything from the most distant stars to the tiniest electron is always in motion, so motion or its velocity (speed), is only relative (this is where the name of the theory of relativity comes from), meaning it

*Einstein never conducted a laboratory experiment in his life. It was all done in his head as thought experiments, and he would then write down his mathematical formulas to prove his theories.*

depends on from where the motion is viewed. This meant that measurement of size, mass, or even time could vary because it depended on the relative motion of the object being measured and the observer doing the measuring.

Einstein applied this same principle of relativity to the velocity of light. Most forms of velocity are also relative. For example, a car approaching a stop sign at 30 miles an hour has a velocity of 30 miles an hour relative to the stop sign or any stationary object. If you throw a ball from the moving car at 20 miles an hour, its velocity relative to the sign is now 50 miles an hour—the speed of the car plus the speed of the ball. Einstein said that light, however, does not act in this way. It always travels at a constant velocity. It doesn't matter if the source of light is moving toward the observer or not. If you are in that same car traveling 30 miles an hour and shine a flashlight ahead of you, the light from the flashlight is still traveling at the same 186,000 miles per second.

Finally, Einstein had some new thoughts on gravity. He said gravity is the same as acceleration in the opposite direction. For example, an elevator accelerating upward has the same effect as gravity pulling your feet into the floor. So, if gravity is the same as acceleration, or motion, and motion affects measurements of space and time, then gravity does, too. This has also been proven in experiments. Clocks tick more slowly when near a mass of gravity like the Sun. Even the angles of a triangle no longer add up to 180 degrees. The effect of gravity changes the measurements.

What did Einstein's theory of relativity mean? First, scientists studying concepts like light, gravity, and energy had many new principles to deal with. Second, it changed our picture of the universe. It was no longer just this huge, expanding box containing different kinds of celestial bodies to fill in the space. The interaction of matter and energy bends space into a curved shape and even affects the flow of time. Time is as much a part of the composition of the universe as matter and energy. The universe is like a four-way dance of matter, energy, space, and time.

*According to Einstein, if you looked through a telescope of infinite strength and no celestial bodies blocked your view, what would you see? Answer: The back of your head.*

*Einstein was offered the opportunity to become the first president of the State of Israel. He declined, saying that being a successful scientist did not qualify him for such a position.*

## Speed Is a Kind of Time Machine

Is there such a thing as a time machine? According to Einstein there is, but you can only travel forward in time. If a spaceship is traveling at the speed of light, time slows down for the spaceship and its passengers. Space travelers who travel to the nearest star system and return to Earth at this speed might have a few years pass by on the ship's calendar, but when they return to Earth they will find that a century has passed. They will have traveled forward in time. According to Einstein, even time is relative; the only constant is the speed of light.

### What was Einstein's involvement in the making of the atom bomb?

As soon as scientists heard the equation $E = mc^2$ in 1905, they knew it was only a matter of time before a weapon of tremendous power would be devised. In 1939, Einstein was informed that scientists in Europe, including Germany, had discovered a way to release the atomic energy of the element uranium. A tremendously destructive weapon would soon be developed based on this discovery.

Einstein was a pacifist who rejected all wars, but the world was in a difficult situation, Adolph Hitler and his Nazi Germany had a plan to conquer the world militarily and to eliminate all Jews. Einstein was born in Germany, but he gave up his German citizenship and escaped to America in 1933 to avoid persecution and probably death.

Other scientists were urging Einstein to inform U.S. President Franklin D. Roosevelt of the development in Europe and to suggest that the United States build such a bomb before Nazi Germany could. It was a very hard decision for Einstein, but when he found that out there had recently been some large shipments of uranium to Germany, he wrote the letter.

On August 6, 1945, the atomic age began. The United States dropped an atomic bomb on Hiroshima, Japan, killing 100,000 and injuring another 100,000. Six hundred city blocks were completely destroyed. The United States had won World War II but Einstein never wanted his discovery to be used in such a way. He worked very hard the rest of his life to make sure that such a weapon would never be used again.

## What is a quantum?

Scientists debated the composition of light for centuries. Did it consist of waves like sound waves? Or was it matter? The Dutch scientist Christiaan Huygens proposed his wave theory of light in the late 1600s and used it to explain reflection and refraction. At about the same time, Sir Isaac Newton suggested that light was composed of small particles he called "corpuscles." In 1868, James Maxwell said that his electromagnetic wave theory applied to light. The answer came in 1900 from the German physicist Max Planck: light has properties of both waves and particles. It was the beginning of modern physics.

Planck proposed that light and all other forms of energy were emitted in small packets he called **quanta** (Latin for "how much"). He said the size and energy of these packets, now called photons, varied according to the wavelength of the light—the shorter the wavelength, the larger the quantum. Light energy is carried by these particlelike photons, and brightness comes from the number of photons arriving at a point at a certain time.

Quantum theory also offered the solution to a mystery about atomic structure. The protons inside the atom's nucleus have a positive charge. To balance them out and give the atom its neutral charge, negative electrons orbit the nucleus. Opposite charges attract—why weren't Bohr's negative electrons attracted toward the positive protons and smashing into them? Bohr used Planck's quantum theory to solve this mystery.

In 1913, the Danish scientist Niels Bohr proposed that an electron only absorbs and emits energy in the fixed amount of a quantum, not as a continuous radiation. This affects the path of the electron's orbit. As the electron emits energy, it assumes a new orbit closer to the atom's nucleus. However, at this level, it is not capable of giving off any more energy. This is why it stays in orbit and does not col-

*Max Planck did not escape Germany during World War II as many scientists did. He stayed in Germany, but he refused to take the Nazi loyalty oath. The last time he refused, they executed one of his sons.*

*After escaping from Nazi rule in Denmark, Bohr worked on the Manhattan Project in the United States to help build the first atomic bomb.*

lapse into the nucleus. As an electron absorbs energy, it assumes another new orbit farther from the nucleus, forming a type of shell around the nucleus instead of a ring, with each shell having a different quantum level.

## Who discovered neutrons?

In 1932, the English physicist Sir James Chadwick discovered that the nucleus of the atom consisted of another particle besides protons. He called the particles neutrons because they had a neutral charge, unlike the positively charged protons. At the time, the discovery did not make many headlines. Rutherford had predicted the neutron's presence many years before as the only possible explanation for some extra weight in the nucleus besides the protons. Within just a few years, an Italian physicist would find a way to turn the neutron into much more than just another atomic particle.

## Who was Enrico Fermi?

Enrico Fermi was born in Rome, Italy, in 1901. His family was poor, and Fermi was so shy that he had few friends. He would spend his time in used bookstores buying as many books as he could on his favorite subjects, math and physics. Throughout his education, he was far ahead of his classmates and even some of his teachers. He attended the University of Pisa and received his doctorate in physics by the time he was 20.

In 1926, Fermi became the director of the school of physics at the University of Rome. The school was making a strong effort to become one of the best physics schools in Europe and was searching for the best minds in Italy. In 1933, French physicists Irène Curie (daughter of Marie) and Frédéric Joliot-Curie discovered a way to produce artificial radioactivity through the use of alpha particles. Fermi decided to investigate this process further. It would lead him into what has been called the greatest experiment of all time.

## How did Fermi split the atom?

The Curies' discovery was a breakthrough, but it was limited to a few elements. Fermi wanted to test all the elements, and he made one other key change. Fermi thought

*During World War II, Italy was an ally of Nazi Germany and passed many anti-Semitic laws. Fermi and his Jewish wife managed to escape Italy when he went to Sweden to accept the Nobel Prize in 1938. They then emigrated to the United States.*

the newly discovered neutron would prove a better "bullet" than the positively charged alpha particles the Curies had used. He thought the neutral charge of the neutron would make it less likely to be repelled by the nucleus of some elements than the alpha particles.

First, Fermi built a simple neutron gun made up of radon and beryllium. The radon shot alpha particles at the beryllium, and this made the beryllium shoot out neutrons. Fermi then went through all the elements one by one. After a couple of months, he had made radioactive forms of many elements. He also discovered that slowing the neutrons down by making them pass through wax or even water increased the radioactivity level 100 times.

Fermi's greatest discovery came next. When neutrons bombarded the nucleus of uranium, the atom would split into two smaller atoms. This process is called nuclear **fission.** There were two more remarkable results from this fission. First, the two new atoms together weighed much less than the original atom—the missing weight was energy. Matter had been converted to energy just as Einstein had predicted. Second, the fission produced more neutrons, and these neutrons went on to produce more fission. As long as there was enough uranium, a chain reaction would result. This meant that products of the

Enrico Fermi sits at the control panel of the "world's most powerful atom smasher" (a particle accelerator) in 1951. Fermi used the particle accelerator to produce nuclear fission and develop workable atomic power plants.

reaction would keep the reaction going. Atomic power was now a reality.

## What was the Manhattan Project?

Fermi's discovery of man-made fission had two implications. If the reaction could be controlled, it would be a new source of tremendous amounts of power to produce electricity. Sustained fission could also produce the most destructive weapons ever made. The nuclear power plants would have to wait—World War II had just started and Nazi Germany was trying to conquer the world.

Many great scientists were escaping from Germany to avoid persecution. Einstein had escaped to the United States in 1933. In 1938, the Austrian physicist Lise Meitner escaped from Germany into Sweden and brought troubling news with her: two German physicists, Otto Hahn and Fritz Strassmann, were working on atomic fission. It was only a matter of time before they succeeded. With this news, the United States decided to set up research into an atomic bomb. The top-secret project was called the Manhattan Project even though the research took place in Chicago, and Fermi was named to lead the research team.

Research centered on whether the reaction could be controlled. If it could, a bomb could be built. Fermi and his team needed to resolve one problem before conducting an experiment. They wanted something even more efficient than water to slow down the neutrons. Water absorbed some neutrons in the process, and they needed every possible neutron for the reaction. Fermi decided that graphite would slow down the neutrons without much absorption.

On December 1, 1942, they were ready. The historic experiment was actually quite simple. A huge atomic pile had been constructed consisting of 6 tons of uranium metal and 58 tons of uranium oxide. Four hundred tons of graphite bricks were placed around the uranium, and Fermi's neutron gun was aimed at the pile. To control the reaction, a few cadmium rods were inserted into the structure. These rods would absorb neutrons as long as they were within the pile. Geiger counters stood nearby to measure the reaction.

*Uranium fission has 20 million times the explosive energy of TNT.*

*The fission of 0.25 gram of uranium yields as much energy as burning half a ton of coal.*

*Huge amounts of energy are also produced by nuclear fusion, when the nuclei of two small masses combine into one large mass. The Sun produces its energy by nuclear fusion.*

Fermi turned on his gun and gave the order for the cadmium rods to be removed. The final rod was removed very slowly. As it was removed, the Geiger counters measured more and more radiation. The instruments then showed that a chain reaction was under way—atomic fission could be controlled. Three years later, an atomic bomb was dropped on Japan (Germany had already been defeated) and World War II was won.

## What did the discovery of atomic fission lead to besides the atomic bomb?

Once the war was over, scientists could concentrate on other uses for this new source of tremendous amounts of energy. Nuclear power plants were built to use fission to produce electricity. There are now over 400 nuclear power plants in the world. France and Sweden produce nearly half their electricity with nuclear power. There are two drawbacks, however, to nuclear power. There is always the possibility of an accident. In 1986, a Russian nuclear reactor exploded, killing 19 people immediately and contaminating a huge area of Russia with harmful radioactivity. Nuclear power plants also produce nuclear waste, which needs to be buried deep underground. The waste remains radioactive for 13 million years.

## He Didn't Know He'd Discovered Fission

When Fermi was conducting his experiments with neutrons and the elements, he was looking for a better, artificial way to produce radioactivity, not nuclear fission. When he got to uranium, he was concerned that its very high level of radioactivity might harm his instruments. He placed a sheet of aluminum foil between the uranium and his Geiger counter. When the experiment was complete, he thought he had found a new element, but he had no idea he had split the uranium atom.

Lise Meitner and her nephew Otto Frisch duplicated the experiment, without the aluminum foil, and realized what Fermi had done. She notified him immediately, and the Manhattan Project was soon under way. Meitner was invited to be part of the project to build the first atomic bomb, but she refused.

Who was Nicolaus Copernicus? ◆ How is the Copernican
system different from the Ptolemaic? ◆ Why was astron
omy so important in Copernicus's time? ◆ What did
Copernicus do with his findings? ◆ Who was Johanne
Kepler? ◆ How did Kepler improve on Copernicus's theory
◆ What other astronomer was instrumental in Kepler's dis
coveries? ◆ What was Kepler's theory of perfect shape
and numbers? ◆ Who was Galileo? ◆ What astronomica
discoveries by Galileo almost got him burned at the stake
◆ What were Galileo's other contributions to science? ◆
Who was Sir William Herschel? ◆ What was unusual about
Herschel's first great discovery? ◆ What were Herschel'

# AMAZING ASTRONOMERS

## Who was Nicolaus Copernicus?

When Christopher Columbus sailed to the New World
in 1492 and proved Earth is a sphere, astronomers started
thinking differently about Earth's place in the universe.
For 1,400 years the Ptolemaic system, with Earth at the
center of the universe and all other celestial bodies
revolving around it in transparent spheres, had remained
unquestioned. The powerful Catholic and Protestant
churches vehemently defended the Ptolemaic view of
man at the center of all things. Some scholars, though,
were beginning to have doubts about Ptolemy's views.
One was about to prove him wrong with one of the most
important scientific discoveries in history.

Nicolaus Copernicus was born in Toruń, Poland, in
1473 into a wealthy family with strong ties to the local
Catholic church. His education was remarkably complete.
At the University of Kraków, he studied philosophy, mathematics, geography, and astronomy. He also studied in
Italy, where he received a law degree, a medical degree,
and a doctorate in church law.

Throughout all his years of study, Copernicus's true
passion remained astronomy. In 1506, he succeeded his
uncle as the bishop of Frauenburg Cathedral in Poland.
Copernicus turned one of the towers of the cathedral into
an observatory. He cuts holes into the ceiling and

observed the movements of the planets and stars. He recorded their position year after year and worked out mathematical formulas to calculate their movement. By 1530, he was sure that Ptolemy was wrong.

*Copernicus had no better instruments than the ancient world had to measure movements in the sky. His observations were still done basically with the naked eye.*

## How is the Copernican system different from the Ptolemaic?

Around 270 B.C., the Greek astronomer Aristarchus proposed that Earth and the other planets revolved around a stationary Sun. He was dismissed as a madman—until Copernicus. Copernicus studied the movements of the planets in the 1,400 years since Ptolemy and found that Ptolemy's idea of epicycles—secondary orbits within the main orbit—could not be true.

Copernicus put the Sun in the center with Earth and the planets revolving around it. This made all his measurements of the planets' movements make sense. The Copernican system explained the changing seasons, the apparent movement of the stars, and why stars appeared and disappeared from the sky. It also supported the idea of Earth rotating on its axis and concluded that the stars must be much farther away than previously thought.

*When civil wars were ruining the Polish economy, Copernicus worked out a new money system for the Polish government.*

Copernicus explained the wandering of the planets in the sky by the different lengths of their orbit around the Sun, not Ptolemy's epicycles. Earth had shorter orbits than Mars, Jupiter, and Saturn, the only outer planets known at the time. Every time Earth seemed to pass these planets in their orbits, the planets would appear to be moving backward.

## Why was astronomy so important in Copernicus's time?

In the early 1400s, a new number system was introduced into Europe from Arabia. The old Greek and Roman systems made calculations very difficult. Using the new Arabic numerals, only 10 different digits were needed to express any number. People at that time still depended on celestial movements to determine medical treatment and to predict the future. Measurements of these movements were now much easier.

At the same time, sea travel was becoming much more important for commerce and exploration. Ships

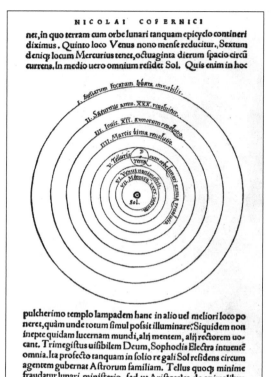

**NICOLAI COPERNICI**

net, in quo terram cum orbe lunari tanquam epicyclo contineri diximus. Quinto loco Venus nono mense reducitur., Sextum deniĝ locum Mercurius tenet, octuaginta dierum spacio circū currens. In medio uero omnium residet Sol. Quis enim in hoc

I. Stellarum Fixarum Sphæra, immobilis.

II. Saturnus anno. XXX. revoluitur.

III. Iouis. XII. annorum reuolutio.

IIII. Martis bima reuolutio

V. Telluris cum orbe lunari annua reuolutio.

VI. Venus nouem[?]

Mercuri[?]

Sol.

pulcherimo templo lampadem hanc in alio uel meliori loco po neret, quàm unde totum simul possit illuminare? Siquidem non inepte quidam lucernam mundi, aliĵ mentem, aliĵ rectorem uo= cant. Trimegistus uisibilem Deum, Sophoclis Electra intuentē omnia. Ita profecto tanquam in solio re gali Sol residens circum agentem gubernat Astrorum familiam. Tellus quoĝ minime fraudatur lunari ministerio, sed ut Aristoteles de animalibus ait, maximā Luna cū terra cognationē habet, Concipit interea à Sole terra, & impregnatur annuo partu. Inuenimus igitur sub
hac

With this simple illustration of the planets orbiting the Sun, published in 1543, Copernicus revolutionized Western science.

were getting larger and traveling farther away from home, sometimes across the vast Atlantic Ocean. The science of navigation was vital to the success of these voyages, and the ships relied on astronomical tables to guide them. Astronomical discoveries were also helping the powerful churches create more accurate calendars so that holy days could be celebrated properly.

## What did Copernicus do with his findings?

Actually, Copernicus didn't do much of anything with them. It took tremendous courage for him to conduct his experiments. He was defying Ptolemy, the church, and common sense. He did not want his discovery to cause any conflict, so when he had finished writing a book on his findings, he kept it hidden for years in one of his desk drawers.

## The Price of Free Thought

The immediate reaction to Copernicus's book was minimal. It opened the eyes of some scientists, but most people continued to believe in the Ptolemaic system, probably because it made humans seem more important. By the end of the 1500s, an Italian scientist and philosopher named Giordano Bruno started to teach the Copernican system throughout Europe.

At the time, the Catholic church was waging a war called the Inquisition against nonbelievers. The church declared Bruno a heretic, or nonbeliever, and ordered him to stop teaching about Copernicus. He refused and was burned at the stake in 1600.

Many other scholars were condemned to similar deaths for teaching the alleged heresy of Copernicus. The great Italian astronomer Galileo (see page 122 for more on Galileo) had been teaching the Copernican system for many years when he was called before the Inquisition in Rome in 1633. He was offered the choice of supporting Ptolemy's views or being burned at the stake. Galileo reluctantly said, "Ptolemy was the correct scholar."

*Another reason Copernicus was reluctant to publish his work was that he knew his calculations were off slightly but he did not know why. The problem was that he did not realize that the planets' orbits were elliptical rather than circular.*

In 1540, the German astronomer Rheticus visited the aging Copernicus and read his book. He realized the importance of it and pleaded with Copernicus to have it published. Copernicus resisted for two more years before relenting. A copy of his *Revolutions* was brought to him on his deathbed, but he was right: the Copernican system would not be completely accepted for another 150 years.

### Who was Johannes Kepler?

As brilliant as Copernicus's theory about the movement of the planets was, he was still wrong about one vital issue: he thought their orbits were perfect circles. The idea that Earth was not the center of the universe and that planetary orbits were not circular was very hard to accept. It was frightening to many people because it challenged humanity's view of itself and God.

Even most scholars were certain of the perfectly circular orbit. Aristotle insisted that celestial bodies were created by the gods and had to move in perfect circles. Ptolemy had apparently proved the shape of orbits with complex mathematical calculations, even adding a second perfect circle. It would take a brave and brilliant scientist to say, "Orbits are not circular," and to prove it.

Johannes Kepler was born in Weil, Germany, in 1571. A severe case of smallpox when he was four left him with poor eyesight and crippled hands. It was clear that he was only suited for a life of learning, and so his family sent him to a seminary to study theology. In his studies, he was introduced to the new ideas of Copernicus and immediately switched his career to astronomy. It was a decision that would lead to the shattering of a 2,000-year-old fallacy.

## How did Kepler improve on Copernicus's theory?

The problem for Copernicus was that even though the circle was accepted as the shape of celestial orbits, careful measurements did not support it. Copernicus was never able to solve the problem, but Kepler had some extra information to work with. In the 60 years since Copernicus's death, astronomers had continued to study the planets' movements carefully. Kepler used these records to try to determine the shape of the planets' orbits.

An engraving of Johannes Kepler shows the great astronomer in his middle age. He had worked with Tycho Brahe earlier in his career, and eventually his reputation surpassed Brahe's.

*Kepler worked out a mathematical formula to describe the physical relationship between the planets. If you square the time it takes two planets to revolve around the Sun, it is proportional to the cubes of their distances from the Sun.*

The task was more difficult than it sounded. He had to determine the path of a planet—Kepler chose Mars—that was moving at an unknown speed in an orbit of unknown shape, and the measurements had to be taken from another planet, Earth, with the same unknowns. After six years of observations and calculations, he still had no answer. He decided to work in reverse—instead of trying to make the numbers fit into a shape, he would see what shape the numbers made. It worked. Kepler finally determined that the orbit's shape was an ellipse. An ellipse is oval-shaped, like a circle with two opposite sides flattened.

This shape also made Kepler realize that some force must be at work to make the planets move in this way. The ellipse showed that planets are sometimes closer to the Sun than at other times. His observations also showed that the planets move more quickly when they are nearer the Sun. He guessed that this force comes from the Sun, and he saw the same force at work in the Moon's orbit of Earth. Kepler had set the stage for the discovery of gravity.

### What other astronomer was instrumental in Kepler's discoveries?

*Kepler was an expert astrologer and increased his income with astrology readings.*

When Kepler started his experiments, he knew he needed the most accurate measurements of the planets' movements available. Tycho Brahe was a Danish astronomer who had his own observatory and the most advanced instruments of the time. He had giant sextants and quadrants and a tool called an equatorial armillary that measured the angles between the stars and the planets.

Brahe's instruments and the meticulous care he took in his work gave him the most accurate observations of the skies that had ever been made. As accurate as his measurements were, however, Brahe still believed Earth to be the center of the universe. He did believe the other planets revolved around the Sun, but thought the whole solar system revolved around Earth at a very great distance.

Kepler was more interested in Brahe's records than his theories, and he was hired to work as Brahe's assistant. Within a year, Brahe died and left Kepler all his notes and calculations. It was the accuracy of these records that

## An Interest in Light and Optics but Not Telescopes

In 1609, Galileo (see page 122 for more on Galileo) announced the discoveries he had made with his first telescope. Kepler was of course fascinated by the idea and wrote the first treatise on optics. His theories were basically correct and are still in use today.

The study also included a discussion of the nature of light and proposed that light is actually made up of a series of colors. Isaac Newton proved this idea many years later in his famous study of light. Despite his interest in this new tool, Kepler never attempted to build a telescope for his own use.

allowed Kepler to make his discovery. As a tribute to his fellow astronomer, Kepler completed Brahe's *Rudolphine Tables,* the first nautical almanac that showed the planetary positions for years to come.

### What was Kepler's theory of perfect shapes and numbers?

Kepler had no trouble combining his belief in science with his belief in God. He believed that God made the universe according to a mathematical plan. This led to his theory of perfect shapes and perfect numbers, something he called "the music of the spheres."

Kepler, like the ancient Greeks, believed in five perfect shapes—the cube, the 4-sided tetrahedron, the 8-sided octahedron, the 12-sided dodecahedron, and the 20-sided icosahedron. He believed the various distances of the planets' orbits could be explained using these shapes. If the shapes could be made to fit into the orbits, then mathematical formulas could be used to calculate all aspects of the orbit.

Kepler was also looking for a mathematical proof of this theory as he studied the shape of the planets' orbits. Of course, he never found it, because there is no scientific basis to the theory. Despite his failure to prove his theory, Kepler continued to believe in it the rest of his life.

*At the height of the witchcraft trials in Europe, Kepler's mother was imprisoned to stand trial as a witch. She was eventually released but died soon afterward.*

*Kepler was the first to propose that Earth's ocean tides were caused by some force from the Moon.*

*Galileo is considered the first experimental scientist because his experiments combined observation, measurement, and reasoning.*

## Who was Galileo?

In 1609, Jacques Badovere wrote a letter to his former teacher telling him of an amazing new instrument from Holland called a "Dutch cylinder." With one convex lens placed in front of one concave lens inside the cylinder, the instrument made distant objects appear much closer. Ships miles away at sea could be seen approaching land.

The teacher was the Italian scientist Galileo, and he immediately understood how important such an instrument could be in astronomical studies. He started building his own stronger telescopes (as they were renamed in Italy) until he had made one powerful enough to see details on the Sun, the Moon, and the planets. The scientific and religious worlds were about to be shaken again.

Galileo Galilei was born in Padua, Italy, in 1564, the same year as William Shakespeare. He was an excellent student, particularly in mathematics, but he was unable to complete his university degree due to a lack of money. Despite this, he was named a mathematical lecturer at the University of Pisa, and by 1609 he had made several important scientific discoveries concerning motion and forces.

Galileo's skill at using a telescope let him gather evidence to support Copernicus's theory that Earth orbited the Sun. Nevertheless, his accurate observations did not prevent his persecution by the Roman Catholic church hierarchy.

Galileo became famous when he dropped two objects of different weights off the top of the Leaning Tower of Pisa and refuted Aristotle's belief that heavier objects fall faster than lighter ones. The demonstration made Galileo famous, but his greatest discoveries were yet to come. Before the invention of the telescope, astronomy had only been a minor interest of his, but what he saw through his telescope would change his life—and the world.

### What astronomical discoveries by Galileo almost got him burned at the stake?

It had been 70 years since Copernicus proposed that the Sun, not Earth, was the center of the universe. The academic world, however, was still teaching the Ptolemaic system, with an unmoving Earth at the center. Most scientists simply did not believe Copernicus's theory; others who did and tried to teach it were burned at the stake as heretics. Galileo understood the dangers of supporting the Copernican system of the universe, but he thought his observations might offer the proof that the church was looking for.

He first turned his telescope on the Moon and saw tremendous mountains and valleys. He calculated some of

## What Time Is It?

As science moved toward experimentation to prove its theories, tools of measurement became vital. The measurement of time was probably the most important of all, but in Galileo's time, scientists had not yet invented a dependable timepiece. Ancient humans could measure years, months, and days with the movements of Earth, the Moon, and the Sun. People in the Middle Ages tried to measure the minutes and hours of the day with a mechanical clock that used gears, wheels, and weights, but these clocks were unreliable.

Galileo discovered that a pendulum always takes the same amount of time to swing whether the swing is narrow or wide. Sixteen years after Galileo's death, the Dutch scientist Christiaan Huygens attached a pendulum to the gears of a mechanical clock, and the grandfather clock was born. Humans finally knew what time it was, and science had a new important tool.

the mountain heights at 4 miles. He saw Venus go through phases like the Moon, but they occurred in a way that he knew could only have been caused by the planet's movement around the Sun.

Galileo saw sunspots clearly enough to study them. Their movement proved that the Sun rotates on its axis. The telescope revealed millions of stars, not 2,000 as previously thought. The haze of the Milky Way, visible to the naked eye, was the glow from these stars. He saw many more stars within known constellations.

Galileo's most amazing discovery was the four moons orbiting Jupiter. This was particularly important because those who rejected the Copernican system argued that the presence of Earth's moon proved that Earth could not be moving. If it were moving, it would leave the Moon behind. Jupiter's moons refuted their theory.

Galileo felt his discoveries proved that the Copernican system was not just a mathematical concept. He went to Rome to demonstrate his telescope to the Catholic church. They were unmoved; some said the telescope must be wrong. The church condemned Copernicus's theory and forbade the publication or reading of his book. Galileo was ordered to reject his beliefs and forbidden to teach them.

*In 1992, the Catholic church acknowledged that its condemnation of Galileo was a mistake.*

Fifteen years later, a new pope was in power. Pope Urban VIII had been a personal friend of Galileo's and seemed sympathetic to scientific thought. Galileo thought the time was right to publish a book on his astronomical beliefs. His *Dialogue on the Two Great World Systems* was published in 1632, but he had misread the church. He was called to Rome again and forced under threat of torture to recant his beliefs from his knees. As he rose, some said they heard him mutter, "*Eppur si muove*" ("But it does not move"). Even though he had recanted his astronomical beliefs, Galileo was still found guilty of heresy and sentenced to spend the rest of his life in seclusion at his home. He died eight years later.

### What were Galileo's other contributions to science?

If Galileo had never looked through a telescope, he still would have been considered a great scientist. His findings on the laws of motion set the stage for the work of Sir Isaac Newton one generation later. He not only proved that weight does not affect how quickly objects fall, he also proved that they accelerate as they fall due to Earth's gravity, or pull. He also worked out the mathematical formulas to calculate the acceleration.

Galileo proposed the concept of inertia, the tendency of an object to stay at rest or in motion until an outside force acts on it. His study of pendulums led to much more accurate clocks. He invented a thermometer to measure temperature. He proved that air has weight and was the first to explain the effect of air resistance.

His most important experiment with motion concerned cannonballs but had significance beyond weaponry. The Italian military hired Galileo to study cannonballs so that they could make more accurate weapons. His experiment was ingenious. He knew he could not study the cannonball while it was in flight, so he used a sloping wedge on the ground. He would push the ball along the top of the wedge and measure its path as it rolled down the wedge. This was the same path the ball would follow in the air if shot from a cannon.

Galileo knew two forces were acting on the ball. Its inertia would make it go in a straight line until Earth's gravity pulled it downward. The resulting curved path is called a parabola. Galileo didn't know it at the time, but the experiment explained the path the planets take around the Sun.

*Galileo was the first astronomer to see Saturn's rings, but he didn't know what they were. He thought they might be satellites, but they disappeared from view too easily for him to be sure.*

## Who was Sir William Herschel?

By the late eighteenth century, the development of the telescope had made it possible for many amateur astronomers to search the skies. Most were content to view what was already known, while some dreamed of great discoveries. One 41-year-old musician in Bath, England, wanted to systematically catalog the whole sky. This amateur wound up making two discoveries that rocked the astronomical world.

Friedrich Wilhelm Herschel was born in Hanover, Germany, in 1738. There was little in his first 35 years to indicate that he would become one of the greatest astronomers to ever study the skies. He came from a musical family and received little education beyond music. When he was 19, Herschel moved to England and changed his name to William Herschel. For the next 17 years, he led the life of a successful musician, writing, teaching, and playing in local orchestras.

In 1773, Herschel held the important position of organist for the Octagonal Chapel in Bath, but his mind was on other things. He had developed a passion for astronomy and had read all the books he could find on the subject. He started renting telescopes, but when they proved unsatisfactory, he built his own. He would see much farther than any man had ever dreamed.

*Herschel discovered more than 800 double stars, now called binaries, and correctly theorized that they revolved around a common center of gravity.*

### What was unusual about Herschel's first great discovery?

By 1781, Herschel had become an expert telescope maker and had built the most powerful telescope in the world. One night while he was working on his catalog of the stars, he saw something near the constellation Gemini that he hadn't seen before. He could tell it was not a star from its movement, so he concluded that it must be a comet.

Herschel charted its movements for the next several weeks and passed on the information to astronomers at England's Royal Society. He was anxious to get back to his catalog. Observations continued at the Society, but there was something wrong with this comet—it had no tail. After several more weeks of observations, the answer was clear. It was a new planet.

*Even Herschel was wrong once in a while. He theorized that sunspots were holes in the Sun's atmosphere that revealed a cool surface beneath—a surface that might even support life.*

Herschel didn't know it, but he had discovered the first new planet since ancient astronomers had viewed Mercury, Venus, Mars, Saturn, and Jupiter thousands of years before. The new planet's orbit around the Sun was calculated at 84 years and its distance at nearly 2 billion miles. The size of the solar system had doubled. Herschel wanted to call the star Georgium Sidas (George's Star) after King George III, but it was finally named Uranus after the Greek god of the heavens. Herschel was made private astronomer to the king and given a royal pension. He was now the most famous astronomer in the world.

## What were Herschel's "island universes"?

It's hard to top the discovery of the first planet since ancient times, but Herschel's next observation was so amazing that few astronomers believed it until it was proven 150 years later.

As telescopes became more sophisticated, astronomers began to see misty objects much farther away that were definitely not stars. They came to be known as nebulae, from the Latin for "clouds." In his cataloging of the skies, Herschel had found almost 3,000 nebulae. Most of them were very similar in appearance. They appeared flat and elliptical like a flattened wheel. They had a bright center with several armlike projections curving outward to their edges. Herschel called them spiral nebulae.

In studying these nebulae, Herschel began to see individual stars and then groups of stars in clusters. He concluded that all nebulae must be vast groups of separate star systems similar to our own Milky Way system. He also thought there must be a tremendous number of these "island universes," as he called them. Herschel had discovered galaxies.

Herschel even theorized that these island universes might have inhabitants who studied their skies and wondered about the universe as we do. His fellow astronomers were not ready for this bold theory, but the telescopes of the twentieth century would prove Herschel right about separate star systems. Even he might have

*During his lifetime, Herschel completed a systematic catalog of the skies four times. He made a physical count of the stars so complete, that it's considered the first scientific picture of the universe.*

# What's Wrong with Uranus?

After Herschel's discovery of Uranus in 1781, astronomers studied the new planet carefully, but something was wrong with its orbit. It went wildly off track, and some scientists even started to question Newton's laws of gravity.

The mystery remained unsolved until 1846, when another planet was discovered in orbit beyond Uranus. English astronomer John Couch Adams and French astronomer Urbain Leverrier each discovered the huge planet whose gravitational pull was influencing Uranus. The planet was named Neptune after the Roman sea god.

A 1799 illustration shows a 40-foot reflecting telescope made by Sir William Herschel. Herschel opened his telescope workshop in 1782, and by his death in 1822 he had created more than 430 of his amazing instruments.

been astounded at the number of galaxies that have been discovered and the vastness of the universe.

*Herschel discovered Saturn's sixth and seventh satellites and Uranus's first two satellites.*

### What was Herschel's day job?

The key to Herschel's discoveries was his telescopes. His desire to see farther and farther into space meant that he had to become an expert in optics as well as astronomy. By 1779, he had built the best collection of telescopes in the world. His best was a 7-foot instrument with a 6-inch mirror that could magnify 227 times. This was the telescope that found Uranus.

After Herschel became private astronomer to the king, the demand for his superior telescopes grew. Orders from astronomers and kings came pouring in. King George bought five of his large 10-footers. Herschel had little choice but to become a professional telescope maker.

In 1782, he opened a workshop near the king's Windsor Castle. His incredible schedule included 12-hour days at the shop followed by eight hours of searching the night skies. Over the years, he built 430 telescopes. If he never had become an astronomer, he would have been famous as a telescope maker.

## How did Friedrich Bessel first measure the distance to the stars?

After William Herschel proposed his theory of "island universes" (galaxies lying far outside our own Milky Way), astronomers became curious about measuring the distance to the stars. In 1838, the German astronomer Friedrich Bessel used improved telescopes and a technique called parallax to prove that the universe was much more vast than even Herschel had imagined.

**Parallax** is the apparent shift in the position of an object when compared to something more distant. If you hold up one finger and look at it through one eye, and then the other, you will see the effect of parallax. In determining a star's parallax, Bessel needed to measure its shift over at least one year. Caculations using Earth's distance from the Sun would then reveal the star's distance from Earth.

In 1792, Giuseppe Piazzi, an Italian monk, discovered a star moving so fast that he called it the "flying star." Its official name became 61 Cygni because it was located in the constellation of Cygnus, the Swan. Bessel decided that since all stars must travel at a similar speed, 61 Cygni's movement must have meant that it was one of the nearest stars to Earth. 61 Cygni also stayed above the horizon almost year-round, so it made an excellent choice for his first parallax experiment.

Bessel chose two stars from the background to serve as the reference points to judge 61 Cygni's parallax. He then measured the angular distance between the stars with his new Fraunhofer telescope, which was so accurate that it could measure the width of a pinhead from a distance of 2 miles. The changes in these two measurements would provide Bessel with 61 Cygni's parallax after a year of viewing.

One complication in calculating 61 Cygni's parallax, or apparent movement, was the star's real movement. Bessel used past observations taken of the star from 1755 and 1830 to find 61 Cygni's rate of travel. At the end of the year, Bessel had his parallax: its apparent movement was 0.3 second of arc. That meant that it was 657,000 times farther away from Earth than the Sun, or 60 trillion miles away! It was a startling discovery to the astronomy world

*The nearest star to Earth is Proxima Centauri. It's only about 25 trillion miles, or 4.3 light-years, away.*

*When Bessel was taking his nightly parallax readings, he repeated each measurement up to 16 times to make certain it was accurate.*

especially considering they knew it was one of the nearest stars.

### Who was Edwin Hubble?

At the start of the twentieth century, the perception of the universe was still limited to Earth's own Milky Way system, which scientists thought measured no more than 20,000 light-years across. William Herschel had theorized 100 years earlier that there were other separate systems far outside our own, but most astronomers doubted this. There were certainly large clusters of stars, called nebulae, but there was no proof that they were separate systems or galaxies.

Two developments at the start of the century would offer proof of a universe no one had dared imagine. First, telescopes were seeing deeper and deeper into space. Mirrors were now up to 100 inches across and the instruments were placed in huge domes on mountaintops for

In this 1949 photograph astronomer Edwin Hubble looks through the Schmidt telescope, with its 42-inch-wide mirror, at the observatory on Mount Palomar.

clear views. Second, a way had been found to measure the distances to the most distant stars. By 1919, the nebula/galaxy debate was raging among astronomers. An American astronomer decided to settle the issue once and for all.

Edwin Powell Hubble was born in 1889 in Marshfield, Missouri. He was a brilliant student and earned a law degree on a prestigious Rhodes scholarship to Oxford University in England. However, his true passion was astronomy, and he returned to school for his doctorate in astronomy. He was immediately hired by the Mount Wilson Observatory in California and set out to find the edges of the universe. His findings would also bring him to the beginnings of creation.

## What are Cepheids and how did Hubble use them to settle the galaxy debate?

The skies are full of variable stars. These are stars that go through a cycle of fading and brightening, so they look like they're winking. Cepheid variables have very quick cycles, some as short as 12 hours. In 1912, American astronomer Henrietta Leavitt discovered a connection between a Cepheid's cycle and its brightness: the slower the cycle, the brighter the star. She didn't know it, but she had just discovered a way to measure the universe.

Astronomers had already determined the distance of many nearby stars through a method called parallax. This method plotted the movement of a star from different locations over many years. The distance of a star could also be determined by comparing its actual brightness (estimated from the length of a star's cycle) to its apparent brightness. Now that astronomers knew the relationship between a Cepheid's cycle and its brightness, they could use the two formulas together to determine how far away the distant stars were.

In 1917, American astronomer Harlow Shapley first used the formulas to determine the size of the Milky Way. He said the galaxy was 300,000 light-years across and that our Sun was not located in the center. His exact numbers turned out to be inaccurate, but the basic idea was correct—we now know that our galaxy is about 100,000 light-years across.

*The Hubble Space Telescope that is carried aboard a satellite in orbit around Earth was named after Edwin Hubble.*

With this knowledge and a new powerful telescope at Mount Wilson, Hubble set out to measure the universe. First, he had to find a "needle in a haystack"—or a Cepheid in a crowded, very distant star cluster. After four years of searching, he finally found a Cepheid in a cluster called Andromeda and calculated its distance. It was one of the most startling discoveries in astronomical history: the star was 900,000 light-years away.

Hubble confirmed his findings with other Cepheids in the same cluster. He then found similar results for two other clusters. Herschel was right; the "island universes" were other galaxies and the universe was immense beyond belief. (We now know that there are about 100 billion galaxies in the universe.) Hubble was not finished.

*Many years before Hubble's findings, the physicist Albert Einstein had theorized that the universe is expanding.*

### What was Hubble's most amazing discovery?

In the nineteenth century, astronomers discovered that studying the light emitted from a star—a study known as spectrum analysis—revealed what elements stars are made of. Changes in a star's spectrum indicate the movement of the star, and analysis could determine the star's speed and direction. It was revealed that stars only appear fixed in the sky because of their great distance from Earth. They are actually moving at tremendous speeds.

At the same time that Hubble was fixing the galaxies' location, the American astronomer Vesto Melvin Slipher

## A Limit to What We Can See

If Hubble's law proves correct for the entire universe, it will help us estimate the age and size of the universe. In fact, the radius of the measurable universe is called the Hubble radius. There is one problem, however.

The galaxies in the outer reaches of the universe move faster and faster. Astronomers have detected galaxies moving around 90,000 miles per second, or half the speed of light. At some greater distance, the galaxies will be moving at the speed of light. That would be the limit to what we can see of the universe, because light from a galaxy traveling at the speed of light could not reach Earth. This means that we could not see it even though it is there.

was using spectrum analysis to determine their velocities. He measured 41 galaxies and found their speed was as staggering as their distance. Their average speed was 375 miles per second, and all of them were moving away from Earth.

Hubble took the experiment one step further. He measured the distance to 24 of the galaxies Slipher had measured and noticed something strange. The farther away the galaxy, the faster it was moving, and the galaxies were moving away from each other at a rate constant to the distance between them. He saw only one explanation: the universe was expanding.

Over the years, Hubble confirmed his findings by measuring 150 galactic velocities. The finding became known as Hubble's law. He also realized that with such distances involved and the time it takes light to travel, observers on Earth are also looking far back in time. For example, light from the Sun takes about eight minutes to reach Earth, so we see the Sun as it appeared only eight minutes before. However, light from the farthest visible stars, 12 billion light-years away, has taken 12 billion years to reach Earth. We see these stars as they appeared 12 billion years ago, or around the time of the birth of the universe.

## What was Hubble's classification system for galaxies?

Hubble's study of galaxies led him to a classification system based on shape and composition into regular and irregular forms. He found that 97 percent of the regular galaxies had elliptical or spiral shapes. He divided spiral galaxies into two types: normal and barred. The arms of a normal spiral stretch out from a central, circular core, while those of a barred spiral stretch out from an elongated, bar-shaped core.

Hubble found only 3 percent of the galaxies he studied to be irregular, or having no regular shape or internal structure. It is now thought that these galaxies lost their shape after a collision with another galaxy. Hubble knew that the system was not exact because some galaxies have the characteristics of two or more different types.

*Hubble delayed accepting a job at Mount Wilson Observatory for three years while he served in the U.S. army during World War I. He also served for six years during World War II as a weapons expert.*

### What is the big bang theory of the universe?

After Edwin Hubble's galactic discoveries, many scientists felt that for the first time in history we understood the key elements of the structure of the universe. In 1922, the Russian mathematician Alexander Friedmann used Einstein's theory of relativity and Hubble's theory of an expanding universe to propose the **big bang** theory to explain the origin of the universe.

Vera Cooper Rubin uses an instrument that measures the changing amount of light from galaxies. Her theory that the universe is composed mostly of "dark" matter that cannot be seen and is poorly understood places her work at the very limit of today's astronomical knowledge.

The theory asserts that the universe started in a state of infinitely high density and temperature. At some point, this infinitely dense and hot matter exploded out into space and time. Scientists cannot yet explain how this so-called big bang took place, but they estimate that it took place around 15 billion years ago. Depending on its mass, the universe will either continue to expand forever or eventually start to contract in on itself. If it does contract, it may be part of an endless cycle of expansion and contraction.

With the big bang theory, many scientists felt that most of the universe was now knowable and explainable. One astronomer had a shocking discovery for them.

### Who is Vera Cooper Rubin?

Vera Cooper Rubin was born in Philadelphia, Pennsylvania, in 1928 and knew from a very early age that she wanted to study the stars. She built her own telescope at 14 and attended Vassar College because her heroine, astronomer Maria Mitchell, had founded the astronomy department there. There were so few graduate schools that accepted female astronomy students that Rubin's education almost stopped there. Fortunately, she was able to earn her graduate degrees at Cornell University and start a career in galactic research. Her discoveries would stretch our views of the universe even farther.

## What was Rubin's first discovery?

Rubin's first discovery was amazing for several reasons. When she made it, she was still just a 22-year-old student from the virtually unknown graduate department at Cornell. When she presented her findings to the American Astronomical Society in 1950, she was practically booed off the stage. Several years after her presentation, however, her findings would be verified.

Like Hubble, Rubin conducted spectrum analysis of galaxies to trace their movements. With spectrum analysis, light from a star passes through a telescope into a spectrograph where a pattern of lines, or a spectrum, is spread out and photographed. The pattern reveals the composition of the star and its movement. Rubin wanted to know if the galaxies at the outer reaches of the known universe were moving relative to each other in any way besides simply outward.

It was still very early in galactic research, so only about 100 spectra (plural of *spectrum*) were available. Rubin studied each one and found that galaxies of the same brightness, and therefore the same distance from Earth, were moving faster in some parts of the sky than in others. Rubin offered no theory to explain this extra motion at the time, but she knew there was one explanation. The galaxies were rotating around a separate unknown center of gravity, just as the planets in our solar system rotate around the Sun.

## What did Rubin discover about the distribution of galaxies in the universe?

The big bang theory states that the present universe was born in an incalculable explosion of matter and gas. Albert Einstein had proposed the idea early in the twentieth century, and Hubble's discoveries about galaxies seemed to confirm it. Rubin's next discovery would raise questions about the theory.

The big bang theory predicted that galaxies would be distributed evenly throughout the universe. In 1954, Rubin

*In 1965, Rubin became the first woman ever to use the famous Mount Palomar telescopes in San Diego, California.*

*Rubin discovered one galaxy where half the stars are rotating in one direction and the other half are rotating in the other direction. The reason why is still unknown.*

## Earlier Astronomers Hint at Missing Matter

Rubin was not the first astronomer to suggest that there was invisible matter in the universe. In the 1920s, the Dutch astronomer Jan Hendrik Oort found that the velocity of stars in our own Milky Way did not conform to Newton's laws of gravity. However, he thought that the problem was in his observations and did not propose any idea of dark matter.

In the 1930s, Swiss astronomer Fritz Zwicky and American astronomer Sinclair Smith reached the same conclusion. They measured the speed of several galaxies and found them to be moving much too fast to be holding together unless there was gravity from other mass present. They called this matter "missing mass."

Also in the 1930s, Albert Einstein and Dutch astronomer Willem de Sitter created the Einstein–de Sitter model of the universe. In this model, they theorized that invisible matter might exist in the universe. They said this matter did not emit electromagnetic radiation and so had not yet been detected.

calculated that galaxies were lumping together in groups. There were more galaxies in some parts of the universe than in others, and they were being carried there by some kind of local current. Again, fellow astronomers dismissed her findings, even though the findings were confirmed in later research. The most startling discovery was yet to come.

### What is dark matter?

In the 1970s, Rubin started what seemed like an innocent experiment with another American astronomer, Kent Ford. She wanted to determine why spiral galaxies differ in structure. She decided to compare the movements of stars near the center of a galaxy with those in the outer reaches of the galaxy. Rubin chose the Andromeda galaxy for her first experiment and conducted spectrum analysis of different parts of the galaxy.

Most astronomers assumed that the mass or matter of a galaxy was concentrated in the center of the galaxy because that's where most of the light appears. According to Newton's laws of gravity, the stars near the inside of the galaxy should therefore move much faster due to the extra gravitational pull of the extra matter.

Much to their surprise, Rubin and Ford found that the stars in the outer reaches of Andromeda were moving at the same speed as the inner stars. They immediately tested other galaxies and found the same results. In some cases, the speed of the outer stars was actually higher. They were moving fast enough to escape the galaxy's gravity, but that was not occurring.

Rubin knew that there was only one possible conclusion, and it also explained her earlier findings on the additional movements of some galaxies. The distribution of light in a galaxy has nothing to do with the distribution of matter. Instead, there are large amounts of mass in the universe that we cannot see. It is called **dark matter,** and it is the gravity from this dark matter that affects the outer stars of the galaxies.

Rubin has analyzed over 200 galaxies. She estimates that 90 percent of the universe might be made up of this invisible matter. What is this dark matter? It remains a mystery for future astronomers to solve.

*Kent Ford built a spectrograph that could photograph a galaxy's spectrum 10 times faster than the previous spectrographs.*

## Who is Stephen Hawking?

By the 1960s there were two theories that tried to explain the origin of the universe. The big bang theory said that there was an immense explosion 12 to 20 billion years ago and that the universe was still expanding outward from that explosion. Astronomers who believed in the big bang said the movement of galaxies in the outer reaches of the universe supported this theory. The other theory, the steady state theory, rejected the idea that a universe could form out of nothingness. It stated that the universe had no beginning or end. As space expanded, galaxies grew apart. As they did, new stars and galaxies formed to fill in the empty spaces that appeared.

The strongest supporter of the steady state theory was the English astronomer Sir Fred Hoyle. He was giving a lecture one day in London when a young physics student from Cambridge University rose to question him. The student informed Hoyle that his math was in error; in fact, his math disproved the theory. Hoyle tried to defend his

*For most of his adult life, Hawking has suffered from motor neuron disease, an incurable muscle disease that confines him to a wheelchair and makes speech impossible.*

Stephen Hawking's startling conclusions about black holes and the big bang theory have captured the public's interest. In 1998, he and his wife visited then-president Clinton at the White House.

theory, but by the end of the conversation, the brilliant student had disproved the steady state theory.

Stephen Hawking was born in Oxford, England, in 1942. The Hawking family had just moved there to escape the World War II bombing of London by Nazi Germany. He was a brilliant student from the start and attended both Oxford and Cambridge Universities. His interest in astronomy led him into a new field called **cosmology.** Now that so much had been learned about the structure of the universe, scientists called cosmologists were trying to explain its origin. Hawking's theories took cosmology to amazing new levels.

### What are black holes?

In the 1960s, English mathematician Roger Penrose came up with the idea of singularity. A singularity occurs when an object becomes smaller and smaller from being crushed but does not lose any matter. Even the atoms and subatomic particles are crushed. The process continues indefinitely until the object is infinitely small and infinitely dense.

Astronomers believed collapsing stars might form a singularity called a **black hole.** A black hole would have unusual properties. Its tremendous density and small size would mean that the force of gravity at the surface is so powerful that anything entering the black hole, even light, would be trapped. Space would bend around a black hole so completely that the result would be either nothingness or a separate universe with unknown physical laws.

Black holes became more of a reality when astronomers started discovering mysterious objects in the outer limits of the universe, some 12 billion light-years away. These objects, called quasars, were producing incredible amounts of energy. Their masses were calculated at 100 million times more than the mass of our Sun. It is now believed that these quasars might be black holes forming from the crushing, or contraction, of entire galaxies.

### What do black holes have to do with the creation of our universe?

Hawking believes that the conditions in a black hole are the key to our entire universe and the big bang theory. In a black hole, matter collapses into an infinitely dense, infinitely small point. Hawking says that if you reverse the process, you have an infinitely dense, infinitely small point—surrounded by nothingness—exploding outward in a big bang.

Hawking has also answered the key question of how a black hole can be detected if it traps everything, even light, within itself. Hawking showed that subatomic particles can escape the creation of a black hole as radiation, and this Hawking radiation has been detected by radio telescopes.

Hawking has calculated that large black holes like the ones created by the collapse of stars, continue to grow denser by capturing matter and energy from the outside. This supports the theory that the universe eventually reaches a point where it starts to contract rather than expand, leading to what scientists call the big crunch. After the big crunch, one universal cycle is complete and ready to repeat. There is a moment of creation in this theory, but one that has occurred an infinite number of times as the cycle repeats.

*Hawking believes that there are also mini–black holes, smaller than the size of an atom. When they emit radiation, they evaporate and explode.*

*Microwave radiation reaches Earth from every direction in the sky. This radiation is believed to be the remnants of the fireball produced by the big bang explosion that created the universe.*

# A Theory of Everything

Like Einstein, Hawking hopes for "a complete, consistent, and unified theory of the physical interactions which would describe all possible observations"—a theory for everything. Sometimes there are contradictions in science's greatest breakthroughs. For example, Newton's theories explained gravity and motion, and Maxwell's theories explained radiation, but the two could not agree on certain properties of light.

A theory for everything must explain four main forces: gravity, electromagnetic force, the strong nuclear force that holds the particles in the nucleus of an atom together, and the weak nuclear force where atoms break down into other particles (radioactivity). The difficulty scientists are starting to have in proving theories of everything is that the amounts of energy needed for experiments cannot be created on Earth. These amounts of energy may exist in only one place: the outer reaches of the universe.

*In 1908, scientist Herman Minkowski showed mathematically that time and space do not exist separately. Astronomers often speak more of a four-dimensional space-time rather than simply space.*

## Could there be more than one universe?

Some cosmologists have taken Hawking's work and proposed that the same black hole process that formed our universe may have occurred more than once to form other universes. They say that structures called **wormholes** might connect our universe to others. These same wormholes might connect different parts of our universe that are millions of light-years apart. Science fiction writers often use wormholes to describe space travel and even time travel.

It is unknown what is inside a black hole, and Hawking has called the space inside them possible "baby universes." His view of the structure of black holes creates the possibility that these baby universes could connect to each other over vast distances. Hawking dismisses the idea that any kind of travel will ever be possible through these wormholes if they do exist. He says the enormous gravitational pull inside would tear apart any matter that enters it.

Who was Georges Cuvier? ◆ What is catastrophism? ◆ Why did Cuvier reject evolution? ◆ Who was James Hutton? ◆ Who was Sir Charles Lyell? ◆ What were Lyell's principles of geology? ◆ What influence did Lyell have on Charles Darwin? ◆ Who was Sir Charles Wyville Thomson? ◆ What was Thomson's ship like? ◆ What experiments did Thomson and the *Challenger* scientists conduct? ◆ What were the findings of the observations and experiments? ◆ Who was Alfred Wegener? ◆ What was Pangaea? ◆ How was Wegener's Pangaea theory finally proven? ◆ What were Wegener's contributions to meteorology? ◆ Who were Louis and Mary Leakey? ◆ What did the Leakeys dis-

# AMAZING EARTH SCIENTISTS

### Who was Georges Cuvier?

People had some strange ideas about fossils when they were first discovered. Some thought that dinosaur bones were the remains of a race of human giants. Even when it became clear that the fossils were the remains of strange, previously unknown animals like mastodons, some thought these animals must still exist in unexplored areas of Earth. One naturalist figured out what they were, and his insight started the science of paleontology, the study of the fossils of prehistoric animals and plants.

Georges Cuvier was born in Montbéliard, France, in 1769. He was able to avoid the violence of the French Revolution by studying outside of France at the Caroline University in Germany from 1784 to 1788. His studies included government, law, science, and anatomy. Anatomy would become a lifelong interest of Cuvier, and it greatly contributed to his understanding of fossils. After serving as a tutor for several years, he was invited by French biologist Étiénne Geoffroy Saint-Hilaire to work at the new National Museum of Natural History in Paris.

Cuvier was active in government throughout his life. Napoleon named him state councilor and inspector-general of public education. After the French Revolution, France's education system needed reorganizing. Cuvier succeeded in improving higher education throughout the

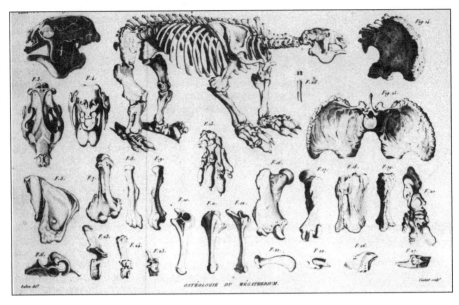

*Georges Cuvier illustrated his work on fossils with his own careful, accurate drawings. His skill as an anatomist allowed him to understand what he drew and to develop the idea that animal species have become extinct throughout Earth's history.*

country and helped found many of France's universities. It was in science, however, that Cuvier made his real contribution, including the discovery of a concept most people of his time found unthinkable: extinction.

### What is catastrophism?

A few scientists before Cuvier believed that fossils were the remains of species that no longer existed, but religion was still a powerful force in science in Cuvier's time. Many scientists could not believe that God would create living things only to wipe them out later. Cuvier decided to settle the issue. For his research, he studied the bones of current-day elephants and the fossils of mammoths that had recently been found. Cuvier was the right man for the job because of his deep understanding of anatomy. He could reconstruct entire skeletons from just a few key pieces.

Cuvier said his findings were indisputable. Not only was the mammoth a different species that no longer lived on Earth, but there were two different elephant species still on Earth, the African and Indian elephants. He confirmed the theory by studying other mammal fossils like the Irish elk and the American mastodon. The fossils were the remains of animals that were extinct, or no longer on Earth. The science of paleontology was born, but what had happened to these animals?

Cuvier made two assumptions to explain extinction. The first was bold and correct: Earth was much older than previously thought. He did not come close to the age of 5 billion years we know today, but he was on the right track. The second assumption was not so correct. He said conditions on Earth were much like the present throughout its very long history. However, once in a while, sudden and widespread catastrophes (Cuvier called them "revolutions") would hit the planet and wipe out a number of species. These catastrophes were natural events, like volcanoes, earthquakes, and floods, and they would also change Earth's landscape. For this reason, he suggested that geologists study these events.

Geologists took Cuvier's suggestion and studied Earth's rock formations. They found Cuvier's theory of catastrophes, called **catastrophism,** to be basically wrong, mainly because Earth was much older than even Cuvier had guessed. Geologists found that features of Earth changed slowly over long periods of time—they called it **gradualism.** Some recent findings have shown Cuvier's theory to be correct sometimes, however. It is probable that the dinosaurs became extinct about 65 million years ago due to a giant meteor striking Earth. The largest extinction in Earth's history took place about 240 million years ago when about 96 percent of all species became extinct. Some evidence points to a meteor being responsible for that extinction also.

## Why did Cuvier reject evolution?

Before Darwin came up with his theory of evolution in 1859, biologists debated how to explain the similarity and diversity among animals, and Cuvier was right in the middle of the debate. Cuvier was brilliant at anatomy, but he made the mistake of dismissing evolution. Both of France's other leading biologists at the time, Jean-Baptiste de Lamarck and Geoffrey Saint-Hilaire, accepted some form of evolution, but Cuvier went in another direction.

The first reason Cuvier rejected evolution was Lamarck's explanation for it at the time. Lamarck said animals pass on to their offspring characteristics they had acquired during their lives. Cuvier did not believe this and the idea was later disproved. The mechanism of heredity,

*Cuvier was asked by Napoleon to become the naturalist on his expedition to Egypt in 1798. Cuvier refused, preferring his research at the Museum of Natural History.*

*Cuvier was the first to correctly propose that life in the sea preceded life on land and that reptiles preceded mammals.*

a strong proof of evolution, had also not been discovered yet, so Cuvier proposed something he called "correlation of the parts."

*Cuvier and Geoffrey Saint-Hilaire engaged in a famous public debate over evolution in 1830 at the Royal Academy of Sciences in Paris.*

Cuvier's theory stated that each species was created for its own special purpose and that each organ or part was created for its own special function. He believed that the form and function of each of the different parts of an animal were an integral part of the whole animal, like the different parts of a clock. No part could be modified without destroying the whole animal. Any change in an animal's anatomy would result in its inability to survive in its environment.

Cuvier believed that all living things had stayed the same from the time they were created. Cuvier found support for this idea by studying the preserved mummies of cats and ibises (wading birds) from Egypt. He showed that they were no different from the cats and ibises of his time despite the passage of thousands of years. He did not realize how slowly the changes of evolution take place.

His emphasis on anatomy in studying animals led him to improve on the popular classification system created by Linnaeus in 1751. He said animals had such diverse anatomy that they could not simply be arranged from simplest to most complex. He added four branches (now called phyla) to the system, each based on a similarity of anatomical structure. Since Cuvier rejected evolution, he said the similarities in anatomy among the animals in each branch were due to their common function, not common ancestry as evolution later said. More changes were made to the classification system after Darwin's theory was pub-

## Playing a Trick on the Professor

One night, Cuvier's students decided to play a trick on their professor. They dressed up in devil's costumes and woke up Cuvier in the middle of the night, chanting, "Cuvier, Cuvier, we have come to eat you!" Cuvier opened his eyes and took a good look at his pretend attackers. He said, "All animals with horns are herbivores [plant eaters]. You cannot eat me," and went back to sleep.

lished in 1859, but Cuvier's idea of phyla is still part of the classification system.

## Who was James Hutton?

In 1795, the Scottish geologist James Hutton wrote a book called *Theory of the Earth*. Hutton had a new theory about how Earth formed. He said Earth was probably millions of years old. He rejected Cuvier's catastrophism and said changes had occurred slowly over these millions of years from simple forces, like erosion and sedimentation, not catastrophes. He said many changes were caused by heat within Earth. He was right on all counts, but almost no one was listening.

Few people read Hutton's book because it was written in a very awkward, unreadable style. It was also written at a time when there was strong belief in a religious theory that Earth was 6,000 years old. Hutton was a farmer whose training had been in medicine—he was an amateur geologist and offered little evidence for his theory. His ideas were unappreciated until a fellow Scottish geologist read them. He would spend decades gathering the evidence Hutton's theory lacked.

## Who was Sir Charles Lyell?

Charles Lyell was born into wealth in Kinnordy, Scotland, in 1797. His father was a skilled botanist, and Lyell, growing up on the family's huge estate, acquired a love for the natural world. His family decided, however, that he would study law at Oxford because science was not considered a "gentleman's" profession. Lyell completed his law degree and practiced for two years, but his mind kept returning to the only course he had enjoyed at Oxford: geology. In 1827, Lyell quit his law practice and started exploring the mountains, dried lake beds, and volcanoes of Europe to gather evidence to prove Hutton right. Just three years later, he wrote *Principles of Geology* and turned geology into a science.

*Lyell was the first to describe the rock cycle. He also invented the term metamorphic rock. These are sedimentary rocks changed by high temperature.*

## What were Lyell's principles of geology?

In 1650, Archbishop James Ussher of Ireland used the history of Earth presented in the Bible to calculate that the world had been created in 4004 B.C. If this were true, how could fossil formations be explained? More and more fossils of plants and animals were being uncovered in thick layers of rock. Sometimes the layers of rock were severely bent. The theory of catastrophism said that when Earth was young, it went through tremendous convulsions, creating mountains, oceans, and other features.

*The theory of gradualism is sometimes also called uniformitarianism because of its belief in uniform laws of change to Earth.*

Lyell looked at the present to see the past. He saw the catastrophes of volcanoes, earthquakes, and floods, but they happened rarely and their effects were limited to relatively small areas. Lyell agreed with Hutton—changes were occurring on Earth all the time and gradually. This theory of gradualism states that over millions of years, gradual effects would seem like a catastrophe. At the time, it was an idea as controversial as evolution because it disputed religious beliefs.

**Lyell revised Principles of Geology 11** *times between 1830 and 1872, as he kept up-to-date on new discoveries in geology.*

Lyell is considered the father of geology because he studied all the changes that take place regularly on Earth and he measured their effects. He studied rainfall and measured how much soil it wears away and carries off. He measured the amount of mud carried by rivers and deposited at their mouths. He measured the amount of lime and other minerals that springs bring to the surface and the amount of land the tides erode.

Lyell used his skills as a paleontologist to further support his theory. He closely studied the fossils that appeared in different rock layers. He saw that the layers closest to the surface, and therefore the most recent, contained fossils of plants and animals that were still living on Earth. The deeper, older layers contained more fossils of extinct species. This discovery led to his calculation of four periods of geologic time, or **epochs,** in Earth's history. He called them Eocene, Miocene, Pliocene, and Pleistocene—terms still used today.

### What influence did Lyell have on Charles Darwin?

Darwin took a copy of Lyell's *Principles of Geology* with him on his around-the-world research voyage aboard the HMS *Beagle*. Darwin was just beginning to formulate his ideas on evolution, and Lyell's findings would have a deep influence on him. There's little doubt that Lyell's basic belief that Earth had undergone gradual changes for

## *Jurassic Park*: **Can the Dinosaurs Return?**

Lyell's most unusual idea in *Principles of Geology* was that the pattern of life on Earth might occur in cycles. Some fossil discoveries were already revealing evidence that huge reptiles (later named dinosaurs) roamed Earth long before humans had. According to Lyell's idea of cycles of life, these reptiles might return one day. Fellow scientists blasted the idea and Lyell eventually retracted it. However, some of today's scientists are wondering if an extinct animal, like a dinosaur, might one day be cloned and brought to life from DNA material found in fossils.

millions of years influenced Darwin's thinking on evolution also.

When Darwin finally published his theory in *On the Origin of Species* in 1859, Lyell became one of his strongest supporters. Darwin had deliberately left out any reference to the evolution of man in his book because he knew the uproar it would cause. Lyell took up that cause by writing *The Antiquity of Man*, showing how man had also evolved gradually over millions of years. In support of his argument, Lyell described some man-made flint tools found in rock layers dating from his Pliocene epoch, over 1 million years ago. Lyell's success with this book encouraged Darwin to publish his similar *Descent of Man* in 1871.

### Who was Sir Charles Wyville Thomson?

For thousands of years, humans navigated the open seas with very little idea of what lay beneath them. By the late nineteenth century, humans knew more about the universe and the atom than Earth's oceans. Early studies of the oceans were primarily concerned with navigation. The oceans were studied to make accurate maps of the world. Lines of latitude and longitude were also calculated for navigation, but there had been little scientific study of the seas.

As late as the 1850s, scientists believed that life could not possibly exist in the depths of the seas below 300 fathoms (1,800 feet). It was a barren, lifeless area they called the **azoic** (from the Greek for "lifeless") **zone.** In

*During one dredging experiment in 1864, scientists found a sea lily that was thought to be extinct. Fossils of it had been found in rocks 120 million years old.*

the 1860s, scientists started dredging (removing the soil or material from the seafloor) at depths below the azoic zone. They found many organisms living below 300 fathoms and they wondered if an azoic zone existed at all. A Scottish scientist led the first of these dredging experiments. Charles Wyville Thomson was born in Linlithgow, Scotland, in 1830. Thomson originally studied medicine, but he became more interested in zoology. He was a professor of natural history at the University of Edinburgh when he became interested in the dredging experiments. In 1870, Thomson asked the British government for a ship for a three-year, around-the-world scientific study of Earth's oceans. The government agreed and the science of oceanography was born. When the study was done, the expedition's naturalist, Sir John Murray, called it "the greatest advance in the knowledge of our planet since the celebrated discoveries of the fifteenth and sixteenth centuries."

*Before the Challenger expedition, many scientists thought the ocean floor was covered with a primordial (meaning "existing from the original creation") slime called bathybius that was the source of all life on Earth. The expedition found the slime to be simply a jelly-like form of calcium sulfate, not living matter.*

## What was Thomson's ship like?

The government provided Thomson with the HMS *Challenger* warship. It was a 200-foot sailing ship, but it was equipped with a 1,200-horsepower engine to power dredging experiments. All but two of the ship's 18 guns were removed and replaced with scientific laboratories and storage space. The ship had a crew of 243, only six of whom were scientists, and it was the first ship specially equipped for oceanographic research. It was about to go on a voyage that would cover about 69,000 nautical miles covering three oceans—the Atlantic, the Pacific, and the Antarctic—and visiting five continents. The *Challenger* embarked from England on December 21, 1872.

## What experiments did Thomson and the *Challenger* scientists conduct?

The scientists on board the *Challenger* were experts in biology, chemistry, geology, and physics, and Thomson's plan for the voyage was very ambitious. They would record data and collect samples at 362 observation stations around the world. Here's a list of the observations and experiments that were performed at most stations:

- The depth of the ocean was measured.
- A sample of material from the ocean floor was gathered for chemical and physical examination.
- Samples of seawater from various depths were gathered for chemical and physical examination.
- The temperature of the seawater was measured at various depths.
- A dredge collected a sample of living things from the ocean floor.
- An adjustable tow net collected a sample of living things from the surface and from medium depths.
- Atmospheric conditions and other weather data were measured and recorded.
- The direction and speed of the surface current were determined. Whenever possible, underwater currents were also measured.

Samples that were not analyzed on board were stored for examination at the end of the expedition. It would eventually take over 100 scientists to complete the work on all the samples Thomson and the *Challenger* brought back to England.

## What were the findings of the observations and experiments?

The *Challenger* returned to England on May 24, 1876. All the oceanographic findings of the *Challenger* expedition would take 20 years to compile into 50 volumes and almost 30,000 pages. Thomson was able to complete a two-volume account of the main findings before his death in 1882.

The most remarkable discovery of the expedition was that many living things existed at the bottom of the deepest parts of the ocean. (The greatest depth they measured was the Mariana Trench near Japan, at 26,900 feet.) There was no azoic zone. Thomson determined that most of these living things were nourished by organic particles from the surface. Dead fish nourished scavengers that also lived on the ocean floor.

The scientists created the first map plotting the ocean's currents and temperatures. They made a map of the deposits of the ocean floor. They discovered the

*Among the supplies taken on the* Challenger *expedition was 144 miles of rope for measuring ocean depths.*

*Of the 243 men who embarked with the* Challenger, *only 144 returned with the ship. Sixty had jumped ship at different ports, 29 had been left ashore due to illness, and 10 had died.*

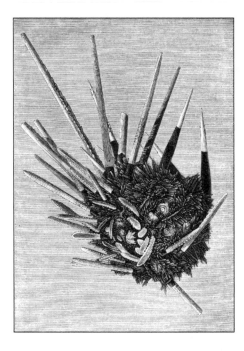

During the 1872–76 voyage of the H.M.S. *Challenger,* the first oceanographic research ship, Charles Wyville Thomson created drawings of sea creatures never before seen by humans.

existence of mountain ranges rising miles above the ocean floor and mapped the main contours of the ocean basins. They discovered an amazing 4,717 new species of ocean life-forms.

## Measuring Ocean Depth and Gathering Samples

Some of the instruments used by the *Challenger* scientists were remarkably simple. Measuring the depth of water is called sounding. Their sounding device was simply a very long rope with a heavy weight (over 100 pounds) attached to the end. The machine lowering the rope had a counting wheel to record the length of rope as it was lowered.

The same idea was used to collect samples from the ocean floor. The weight at the end of the sounding device was a hollow cylinder. When the cylinder hit bottom, it would fill with material from the seafloor. When the device was pulled back to the surface, special wires attached to the cylinder would close the cylinder so that none of the sample was lost. Their water sampler worked on the same principle.

The findings of the expedition contributed to both navigation and science. The shipping and fishing industries benefited from the findings on currents and meteorology. The new maps of the ocean floor aided the laying of telegraph cables across the Atlantic and Pacific Oceans. More expeditions would follow, and oceanography, a blend of biology, chemistry, geology, and physics, would become a very important part of twentieth-century science.

## Who was Alfred Wegener?

In 1596, the Flemish mapmaker Abraham Ortelius proposed a strange theory. He suggested that all the continents of Earth were once joined together and had drifted apart over the course of time due to earthquakes and floods. He offered no evidence other than that the coastlines of Africa and South America seemed to fit together like two pieces of a puzzle. There weren't many geologists around at the time, so the theory was basically ignored.

Three hundred years later, a German meteorologist also noticed the matching coastlines. He then read about an unusual discovery in Greenland. Fossils of some tropical plants were found beneath the Greenland ice cap. How could this be? Did Earth's climate change that dramatically over the years? He researched further and found that there were landscapes in the tropics of Africa and South America that were clearly formed by ancient glaciers. He vowed to prove Ortelius right, with an idea called **continental drift,** a theory that said the continents started moving apart about 200 million years ago.

Alfred Lothar Wegener was born in Berlin, Germany, in 1880. From an early age, he had an interest in two things: astronomy and the polar ice cap. He earned a doctorate in astronomy in 1905 from the University of Berlin but immediately became more interested in meteorology and geology. Wegener would become a great meteorologist, but it was his stand on the origin of the continents that got him the most attention. There were many geologists around by the early 1900s, and almost all of them rejected Wegener's "crazy" theory. One called it "utter, damned rot!" The ridicule would not keep Wegener's theory from revolutionizing earth science.

This photograph of Alfred Wegener was taken in 1929, 14 years after he published his theory of continental drift. Not until the 1960s, after Wegener's death, was the mechanism of continental drift explained.

*One year after Wegener died, English geologist Arthur Holmes published his idea that the continents had been "carried" by larger pieces of Earth's crust. He thought that currents of heat from beneath the crust fueled the movement. His idea was also dismissed until the 1960s.*

## What was Pangaea?

Wegener was so sure of his theory on the origin of the continents that he gave the original continent a name—Pangaea (from the Latin for "all of Earth"). In his research, he found much more support for the theory, in addition to the fossil findings in Greenland. He created a map of Pangaea and found that many geological features from current-day Earth matched up. For example, the Appalachian Mountains in North America matched up with the Scottish Highlands. He also found coal deposits matching up and running uninterrupted across two continents. An unusual kind of rock stratum was found oceans apart in South Africa and Brazil.

Wegener found that more examples of fossils from one climate were uncovered in a totally different climate. He didn't believe Earth's climatic changes could explain this. Other fossils revealed that identical plants and animals lived in both South America and Africa hundreds of millions of years ago. Wegener said his theory also explained the placement of mountain ranges on Earth. Mountain ranges often occur in narrow bands at the edges of continents. Wegener said that they formed as the drifting landmasses collided, such as the Himalayas, which formed where India collided with Asia.

The explanation scientists had previously offered for the similarities between continents was that large "land bridges" had once connected them. The bridges had sunk into the sea as Earth cooled and contracted. Wegener refuted this idea with the accepted concept of isostasy. Isostasy is the movement of landmasses up and down to maintain equilibrium. He said if these "land bridges" had broken up and sunk from some force, they would have risen again in another form when the force was released.

Wegener published his findings in 1915 in a book called *The Origin of Continents and Oceans.* His idea of floating continents drifting apart caused a tremendous uproar in the scientific world. He was attacked as a meteorologist whose training was in astronomy, not a geologist. Despite all the evidence Wegener presented, his critics did have one good argument against him. He could not identify the force or forces that had moved the continents. The technology to identify those forces had not been invented yet. He knew this was the one weakness of his theory. He said, "The complete solution of the problem of forces will be a long time coming." The proof would come, however.

### How was Wegener's Pangaea theory finally proven?

Without the ultimate proof of the force behind continental drift, Wegener's theory was rejected by most as a fairy tale. The first hint of proof came right after Wegener's death, with the confirmation of the submerged mountain range called the Mid-Atlantic Ridge under the Atlantic Ocean and a central valley along its crest. Wegener probably would have concluded that this was evidence of the force he was looking for. The mountain range indicated expansion from under the ocean floor, most likely caused by heat, and the valley indicated a stretching of the ocean floor.

In the mid-1960s, scientists were able to study Earth's crust more closely, especially the ocean floor, and discovered that Earth's outer shell is made up of large, rigid

*Scientists can now map past plate movements much more precisely than before. Using satellites, they can also measure the speed of continental plate movement.*

*India moves north at a rate of 2 inches per year as it collides with Asia. Current plate movement is also making the Atlantic Ocean larger and the Pacific Ocean smaller by a few inches per year.*

plates that move. The concept is called **plate tectonics.** We now know that continents and the ocean floor form plates that seem to float on the underlying rock. The underlying rock is under such tremendous heat and pressure that it behaves like a liquid.

Wegener said whatever the force was behind continental drift, it would also explain the formation of mountains, earthquakes, volcanoes, and other geological features. The idea of plate tectonics explains all of these. Where plates collide, great mountain ranges are pushed up. If one plate sinks below another, chains of volcanoes are formed. Earthquakes usually form along plate boundaries.

### What were Wegener's contributions to meteorology?

Just as Wegener was getting his degree in astronomy, the new science of meteorology was getting a boost from some new scientific advances. The telegraph, the laying of the Atlantic cable, and wireless communications were making storm tracking and weather forecasting much more accurate. Wegener became a meteorologist. He used

## The Final Expedition to Greenland

Wegener conducted four expeditions to Greenland to study its atmosphere and ice cap. On the second expedition, he completed the longest crossing of an ice cap ever made on foot (750 miles). The fourth expedition, in 1930, was to establish three weather stations on the island. One station on the west coast was set up without a problem, but bad weather was holding up progress on the inland station, 250 miles away.

Winter was approaching and the crew desperately needed more supplies. Wegener led a relief party including 13 Greenlanders to deliver the supplies. The weather was so bad that all but one of the Greenlanders returned to home base. Temperatures reached as low as –60°F. It took 40 days to cover the 250 miles, but Wegener was able to deliver the supplies. He set out a couple of days later for the return trip to home base, but he did not make it. He died halfway back, probably from a heart attack.

kites and balloons to study the upper atmosphere. In 1906, he was invited to join an expedition to Greenland's Arctic area as its meteorologist. On the expedition, he became the first person to track the movements of polar storms.

Wegener also became an expert in climatology—the study of a region's weather over a long period of time—and he used it to support his Pangaea theory. He created maps of Pangaea, including ancient deserts, jungles, and ice sheets, and compared them to current-day climatology maps. On the current-day map he saw evidence of an ice age from about 280 million years ago scattered all over Earth, even in the deserts. On his ancient map, all this evidence was packed together in an area around the South Pole.

*Wegener and his brother once broke the world record for staying aloft in a hot-air balloon—for 52 hours.*

## Who were Louis and Mary Leakey?

In the nineteenth century, scientists discovered that Earth was much older than previously thought. Humans and other animals had been on Earth much longer also. Some animals had lived on Earth before humans and become extinct. This raised many questions. How old was Earth? When did life start? When did humans appear?

In 1925, Australian anthropologist Raymond Dart discovered a fossil of a small skull in Taung, South Africa. Dart, also an anatomist, studied the unusual skull carefully. He decided it was a child's skull and the first fossil of a human ancestor. Dart called the fossil *Australopithecus africanus,* from the Latin meaning "southern ape from Africa." (Scientists now refer to all the earliest human species as **australopithecines,** or australopiths for short.) For decades, almost no one in the scientific community believed Dart, but more and more archaeologists started coming to Africa, the place where Darwin had predicted that human life originated. The search for humans' prehistoric ancestors was under way.

It was a husband-and-wife team who would make archaeology front-page news and bring humans closer to understanding their beginnings. He was well educated, brilliant, and sometimes made outrageous claims about their discoveries. She never even finished high school but trained herself as an expert archaeologist and would quietly make most of their discoveries.

Louis Seymour Bazett Leakey was born to missionary parents in Nairobi, Kenya, in 1903 and was raised among the Kikuyu tribe. He returned to England in 1922 to complete his education and received a doctorate in anthropology from Cambridge University. In 1926, he led an expedition to Olduvai, a river gorge in Tanzania, Africa. It was here that he would make his most important discoveries over the next 30 years.

Mary Nicol Leakey was born in London, England, in 1913 but spent most of her childhood traveling with her artist parents. Her father was interested in archaeology and would take her along when he was invited to join archaeological digs in Europe. When she dropped out of school, she joined digs as an assistant to gain experience. In 1935, she joined the Leakey expedition in Olduvai and married Louis the following year. Together, they would make the key archaeological discovery of the twentieth century: humans and their ancestors have been around much longer than was thought.

Mary and Louis Leakey, a husband-and-wife team of archeologists, worked in Africa, where they discovered some of the earliest human fossils in existence.

## What did the Leakeys discover about humans' ancestors?

There are four main developments in human evolution that led to today's *Homo sapiens:* walking on two legs instead of four; a larger, more complex brain; the making of tools; and language. The development of all but language could be revealed by studying fossils of hominids (members of the family that include humans and apes). Other indications of humans' ancestors are teeth and fingers, especially a flexible thumb.

The Leakeys spent many years in Africa studying Stone Age fossils, but they made no major discoveries concerning their favorite area of interest, human origin. That would change in 1948. Mary Leakey found teeth and bone fragments of a skull and was able to piece them together. When she was done, she had the first perfectly preserved skull of a hominid. Only bits and pieces of the species had been found before. The skull was determined to be about 20 million years old, and Louis Leakey called it *Proconsul africanus.* This was not the common ancestor to apes and humans the Leakeys were searching for, but it was a link to those ancestors—its skull revealed that a larger brain was developing.

In 1959, Mary Leakey found an australopith skull, the first to be found in eastern Africa. The Leakeys nicknamed it Zinj (from its scientific name, *Zinjanthropus boisei*) and dated it at about 1.75 million years old. Simple stone tools were also found in the area, but they determined that this australopith was not a toolmaker. The skull did indicate a larger brain than those of ape fossils, and the teeth were also much more like a human's. The Leakeys thought they might have found a direct ancestor, but other archaeologists disagreed. It soon became apparent that there were several different australopith species dating between 4 million and 2 million years ago. Some probably lived on Earth at the same time. Over many years, most of the species died out, but it's likely that at least one of them evolved into humans. It's even possible that more than one evolved into humans separately in a process called parallel evolution.

*The age of fossils is determined by measuring their radioactive contents. Each radioactive element has its own rate of decay, which can be measured. This method is called radiometric dating.*

## The Differences between All the "-ologies"

Once scientists realized that fossils were a key to uncovering Earth's past, the search was on for more, older fossils. Three main new sciences grew out of these studies—paleontology, archaeology, and anthropology.

Paleontology is the study of fossils, including those of humans, animals, and plants. Archaeology is the study of past human culture and behavior; it includes the study of human fossils as well as the man-made materials they left behind, like tools and buildings. Anthropology is the study of all human culture and behavior from the past to the present. Fields of study like anthropology are sometimes called social sciences because the emphasis is the study of human behavior rather than of natural phenomena.

*One of Mary Leakey's first jobs was illustrating archaeology books. She once traced, redrew, and painted 1,600 figures from Stone Age caves for her book* **Africa's Vanishing Art.**

Mary Leakey preferred making the discoveries to joining the debate, and she made one more remarkable find in 1978. It was simply a set of footprints. Erosion had recently revealed an area of stone with imprints of raindrops and animal prints. The animals had walked in it long ago when it was volcanic ash damp from rain. One set of prints was clearly hominid and included a large male, a smaller female, and a child walking behind them, often placing his footsteps in theirs. The prints showed that this species was walking on two feet, one of the developments toward the human species. The date of the prints surprised the Leakeys—they were about 3.7 million years old. This meant that our ancestors were walking upright much sooner than was previously thought.

### What was Leakey's greatest find?

In 1960, Louis Leakey found the skull, leg, foot, and hand bones of another hominid. It was dated at around 2 million years old, just slightly older than Zinj. The bones showed that this ancestor walked on two feet and had a large brain, but there were differences. The teeth were even more similar to human teeth and the hands were different from ape hands, which were designed for strength to swing on tree branches. The thumb was in position to give the hand more control of its grip. (It's called an opposable thumb.) In other words, it was a toolmaker. This was the species responsible for the tools they found with Zinj.

The meaning was clear to Louis Leakey: this species was much more human than ape. He named it *Homo habilis,* meaning "handyman," and claimed that it was the first true human species. He said the Zinj species had died out while *Homo habilis,* with its new toolmaking ability, survived to become the first ancestor of humans.

Some archaeologists again disagreed with Leakey. They said there was still much more to be discovered before declaring *Homo habilis* the first human ancestor. However, there is agreement among archaeologists that the evolution from ape to human took place in several australopith species that lived between 4 million and 2 million years ago. There is still much to be discovered. Archaeology is, after all, a very young science—it's still less than 100 years since Raymond Dart found that first hominid skull.

*Olduvai Gorge, the site where the Leakeys found so many of their fossils, is now in ruins. After the publicity of the fossils found there, the place was overrun by souvenir seekers*

# Amazing Scientists Timeline

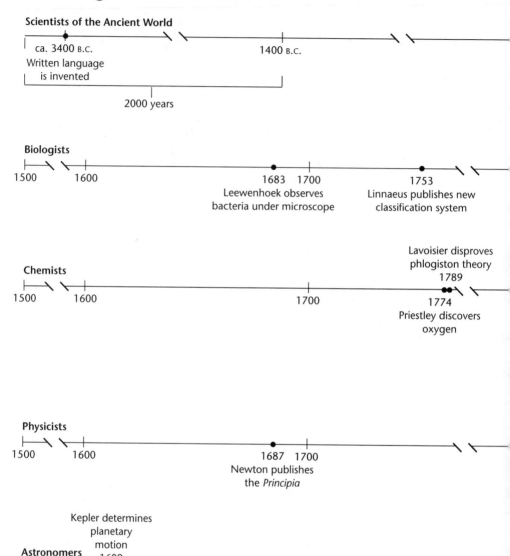

**Scientists of the Ancient World**

ca. 3400 B.C.
Written language
is invented

1400 B.C.

2000 years

**Biologists**

1500    1600

1683   1700
Leewenhoek observes
bacteria under microscope

1753
Linnaeus publishes new
classification system

**Chemists**

1500    1600

1700

Lavoisier disproves
phlogiston theory
1789

1774
Priestley discovers
oxygen

**Physicists**

1500    1600

1687   1700
Newton publishes
the *Principia*

**Astronomers**

Kepler determines
planetary
motion
1609

1500    1600    1633
Galileo forced to
recant Copernican
system

1542
Copernicus
disproves
Ptolemaic system

1700

1781
Herschel
discovers
Uranus

**Earth Scientists**

1500    1600    1700

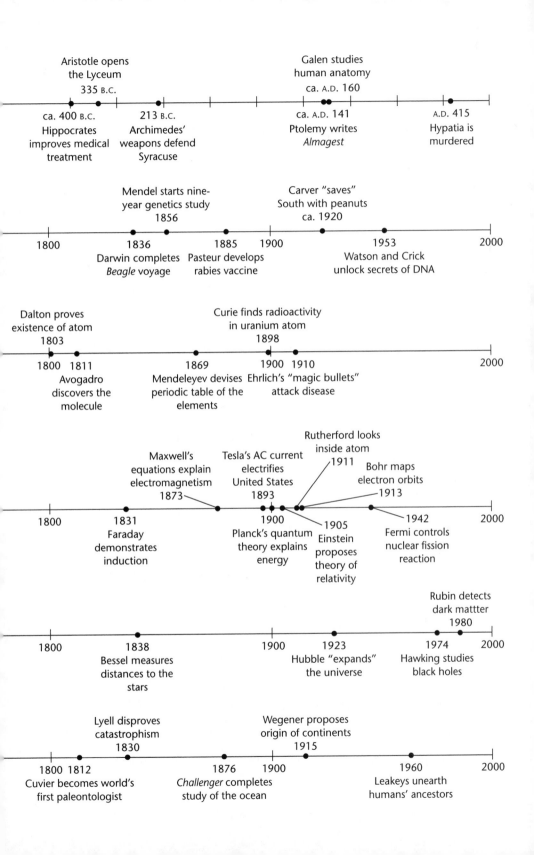

Aristotle opens
the Lyceum
335 B.C.

ca. 400 B.C.
Hippocrates
improves medical
treatment

213 B.C.
Archimedes'
weapons defend
Syracuse

Galen studies
human anatomy
ca. A.D. 160

ca. A.D. 141
Ptolemy writes
*Almagest*

A.D. 415
Hypatia is
murdered

Mendel starts nine-
year genetics study
1856

Carver "saves"
South with peanuts
ca. 1920

1800      1836      1885    1900               1953              2000
        Darwin completes  Pasteur develops        Watson and Crick
        *Beagle* voyage   rabies vaccine          unlock secrets of DNA

Dalton proves
existence of atom
1803

Curie finds radioactivity
in uranium atom
1898

1800   1811              1869         1900  1910                    2000
       Avogadro      Mendeleyev devises  Ehrlich's "magic bullets"
       discovers the  periodic table of the  attack disease
       molecule        elements

Maxwell's
equations explain
electromagnetism
1873

Tesla's AC current
electrifies
United States
1893

Rutherford looks
inside atom
1911

Bohr maps
electron orbits
1913

1800      1831                1900        1905      1942          2000
        Faraday          Planck's quantum  Einstein  Fermi controls
        demonstrates     theory explains   proposes  nuclear fission
        induction        energy            theory of reaction
                                           relativity

Rubin detects
dark mattter
1980

1800      1838              1900     1923     1974          2000
        Bessel measures              Hubble "expands"  Hawking studies
        distances to the             the universe      black holes
        stars

Lyell disproves
catastrophism
1830

Wegener proposes
origin of continents
1915

1800  1812              1876    1900               1960          2000
Cuvier becomes world's  *Challenger* completes     Leakeys unearth
first paleontologist    study of the ocean         humans' ancestors

# GLOSSARY

## A

**alternating current (AC)**   an electric current in which voltage is controlled by alternating its direction of movement

**anatomist**   a scientist who studies the structure of animals or plants

**antibodies**   chemicals in blood that attack disease cells

**antigens**   protein molecules in foreign bodies, like bacteria, that are attacked by antibodies

**antiseptic**   germ free

**astrolabe**   an ancient tool of astronomy used to measure the position of the stars

**astrology**   the study of the planets and other celestial bodies in the belief that they have an influence on human affairs

**australopithecine**   any of a prehistoric species of primates believed to be humans' first ancestors

**azoic zone**   a barren, lifeless area scientists erroneously believed to exist in the ocean depths

**azote**   the original name for nitrogen, from the Greek for "no life" because it did not support combustion

## B

**big bang**   the theory that the universe was born billions of years ago in a huge explosion of matter and gas

**binomial nomenclature**   a two-name system of classifying animals and plants; e.g., *Homo sapiens*

**black hole**   an infinitely small and dense celestial body with tremendous gravitational pull, probably a collapsing star

## C

**calculus**   a system of mathematics used to measure infinitesimal and changing quantities

**capillaries**   tiny vessels that carry blood from the arteries to the veins

**catastrophism**   the erroneous theory that Earth's surface was formed from a series of catastrophic events, like volcanoes, earthquakes, floods, etc.

**chromosomes**   threadlike structures that contain chemical information on how cells are to develop

**continental drift**   a theory that asserts that the continents started moving apart about 200 million years ago

**cosmology**   the study of the origins of the universe

## D

**dark matter**   huge amounts of mass in the universe that cannot be seen

**displacement**   the volume of fluid displaced, or forced to move, by a floating object

## E

**epoch**   a long period of time in Earth's formation based on geological events

## F

**fission**   a nuclear reaction where the nucleus of an atom is split into fragments, producing tremendous amounts of energy

**fluorescence**   the glowing of materials when exposed to ultraviolet light

## G

**galvanometer**   an instrument that detects electricity

**gradualism**   the theory that Earth's surface formed slowly over long periods of time from gradual processes like erosion, sedimentation, etc.

## H

**half-life**   the length of time needed for half the atoms in a radioactive element to decay

**Hippocratic oath**   a code of ethics for physicians to follow in the treatment of patients, from a volume of writings called the Hippocratic Collection but probably not written by Hippocrates himself

**hybrid**   an organism produced by breeding parents that have different forms of the same trait

## I

**immune**   resistant to disease, often by the injection of weak disease cells

**induction**   the conversion of magnetism to electricity

**inertia**   the tendency of an object at rest to stay at rest and an object in motion to remain in motion until acted upon by an external force

## L

**luminiferous**   able to carry light

## M

**mechanics**   the study of the effect of forces on matter

**microbe**   a living thing visible only under a microscope

## N

**natural selection**   the evolutionary theory that plants and animals survive by passing on desirable traits to their offspring, also called **"survival of the fittest"**

**nucleotide**   a DNA compound composed of sugar, phosphate, hydrogen, and one of four bases

## P

**parallax**   an apparent shift in the position of an object when viewed from two points

**pasteurization**   the process of heating liquids to destroy harmful germs, named after Louis Pasteur

**pathology**   the study of diseased body tissue

**phlogiston**   a substance formerly thought to explain fire, disproven by the chemist Antoine-Laurent Lavoisier

**pi**   a ratio of the circumference of a circle to its diameter, used in many mathematical calculations

**plate tectonics**   the movement of huge, rigid plated in Earth's outer shell

## Q

**quantitative science**   using measurements to support theories

**quantum** (plural **quanta**)   an indivisible unit of energy

## R

**reflect**   to bounce waves, like light and sound, off a surface

**refract**   to deflect waves, like light and sound, as they pass from one medium to another

**relativity**   the theory that the measurement of size, mass, and time varies depending on the motion of the object being measured and the observer

**scientific method**   the basic steps of scientific research

## S

**spontaneous generation**   an erroneous theory held before the discovery of the microscope that asserted that lower forms of life originated from nonliving matter

**survival of the fittest**   see **natural selection**

## T

**taxonomy**   a system of classifying organisms into different categories based on similarities

## W

**wormhole**   theoretically, a connection between different universes or distant parts of our universe

# SELECTED BIBLIOGRAPHY

Anderson, Margaret, and Stephenson, Karen. *Scientists of the Ancient World.* Enslow, 1999.

Asimov, Issac. *Asimov's Chronology of Science and Technology.* HarperCollins, 1994.

Bruno, Leonard. *Science and Technology Breakthroughs: From the Wheel to the World Wide Web.* Gale, 1997.

Camp, Carole Ann. *American Astronomers.* Enslow, 1996.

Curtis, Robert. *Great Lives: Medicine.* Atheneum, 1993.

Faber, Doris, and Harold Faber. *Great Lives: Nature and the Environment.* Atheneum, 1991.

Fox, Karen. *The Chain Reaction.* Franklin Watts, 1998.

Hawking, Stephen. *The Illustrated Brief History of Time.* Bantam, 2001.

Hellemans, Alexander, and Bryan Bunch. *The Timetables of Science.* Simon & Schuster, 1991.

Henderson, Harry. *The Importance of Stephen Hawking.* Lucent, 1995.

Lomask, Milton. *Great Lives: Invention and Technology.* Atheneum, 1992.

Martell, Hazel Mary. *The Kingfisher Book of the Ancient World.* Kingfisher, 1995.

Meadows, Jack. *The Great Scientists.* Oxford, 1998.

Mulcahy, Robert. *Diseases: Finding the Cure.* Oliver, 1996.

Nardo, Don. *Scientists of Ancient Greece.* Lucent, 1999.

Parker, Steve. *Albert Einstein and Relativity.* Chelsea House, 1995.

Porter, Roy, and Marilyn Baily Ogilvie, eds. *The Biographical Dictionary of Scientists.* Oxford, 2000.

Poynter, Margaret. *The Leakeys.* Enslow, 1997.

Proffitt, Pamela, ed. *Notable Women Scientists.* Gale, 1999.

Silver, Brian. *The Ascent of Science.* Oxford, 1998.

Simonis, Doris, ed. *Lives and Legacies: An Encyclopedia of People Who Changed the World—Scientists, Mathematicians, and Inventors.* Oryx, 1998.

Stille, Darlene. *Extraordinary Women Scientists.* Children's Press, 1995.

Strahler, Arthur. *Understanding Science: An Introduction to Concepts and Issues.* Prometheus, 1992.

Wilkinson, Philip. *Scientists Who Changed the World.* Chelsea House, 1994.

# THE NEW YORK PUBLIC LIBRARY'S RECOMMENDED READING LIST

Adair, Gene. *George Washington Carver.* New York: Chelsea House, 1989.

Brodie, James Michael. *Created Equal: The Lives and Ideas of Black American Innovators.* New York: Morrow, 1993.

Christianson, Gale E. *Isaac Newton and the Scientific Revolution.* New York: Oxford, 1996.

Foster, Leila Merrell. *Benjamin Franklin, Founding Father and Inventor.* Springfield, N.J.: Enslow, 1997.

Grey, Vivian. *The Chemist Who Lost His Head: Antoine Laurent Lavoisier.* New York: Coward, McCann, & Geoghegan, 1982.

*The Grolier Library of Scientific Biographies.* Danbury, Conn.: Grolier Educational, 1997.

Guillen, Michael. *Five Equations That Changed the World.* New York: Hyperion, 1995.

Ipsen, D. C. *Archimedes, Greatest Scientist of the Ancient World.* Hillside, N.J.: Enslow, 1998.

Klare, Roger. *Gregor Mendel: Father of Genetics.* Springfield, N.J.: Enslow, 1997.

McGrayne, Sharon Bertsch. *Nobel Prize Women in Science.* Secaucus, N.J.: Carol Publishing Group, 1998.

MacLachlan, James H. *Galileo Galilei: First Physicist.* New York: Oxford, 1997.

Olesky, Walter G. *Hispanic-American Scientists.* New York: Facts on File, 1998.

Sherrow, Victoria. *Great Scientists.* New York: Facts on File, 1992.

Stefoff, Rebecca. *Charles Darwin and the Evolution Revolution.* New York: Oxford, 1996.

Yount, Lisa. *Asian-American Scientists.* New York: Facts on File, 1998.

Yount, Lisa. *A to Z of Women in Science and Math.* New York: Facts on File, 1999.

# INDEX

Note: Page numbers in *italics* indicate illustrations.

# PHOTOGRAPHY CREDITS

**Note:** *The General Research Division and The Rare Books Division are part of the Humanities and Social Sciences Library of The New York Public Library (NYPL).*

p. iv, Rare Books Division, NYPL; p. 5, Rare Books Division, NYPL; p. 14, Rare Books Division, NYPL; p. 16, General Research Division, NYPL; p. 20, General Research Division, NYPL; p. 24, Mansell Collection; p. 28, Science, Industry and Business Library, NYPL; p. 31, General Research Division, NYPL; p. 35, WM. B. BECKER COLLECTION/ PHOTOGRAPHY MUSEUM.COM; p. 39, Hulton/Archive/Getty Images; p. 44, General Research Division, NYPL; p. 47, Culver Pictures; p. 53, Courtesy of Cold Spring Harbor Laboratory Archives; p. 58, General Research Division, NYPL; p. 63, Science, Industry and Business Library, NYPL; p. 68, General Research Division, NYPL; p. 73, General Research Division, NYPL; p. 74, Library of Congress Prints and Photographs Division; p. 75, The Stonesong Press; p. 77, AIP Emilio Segrè Visual Archives; p. 81, General Research Division, NYPL; p. 86, General Research Division, NYPL; p. 90, Hulton Getty/Archive photos; p. 95, Science, Industry and Business Library, NYPL; p. 97, Hulton/Archive/Getty Images; p. 102, AIP Emilio Segrè Visual Archives, courtesy Otto Hahn and Lawrence Badash; p. 106, Courtesy of the Archives, California Institute of Technology; p. 112, AP/Wide World Photos; p. 117, Rare Books Division, NYPL; p. 119, Hulton/Archive/Getty Images; p. 122, General Research Division, NYPL; p. 128, Science, Industry and Business Library, NYPL; p. 130, Courtesy of the Archives, California Institute of Technology; p. 134, Carnegie Institute of Washington, D.C.; p. 138, Clinton Presidential Materials Project; p. 142, General Research Division, NYPL; p. 150, Science, Industry and Business Library, NYPL; p. 152, Science, Industry and Business Library, NYPL; p. 156, Bettmann/CORBIS